1 MONTH OF
FREE
READING

at

www.ForgottenBooks.com

By purchasing this book you are eligible for one month membership to ForgottenBooks.com, giving you unlimited access to our entire collection of over 1,000,000 titles via our web site and mobile apps.

To claim your free month visit: www.forgottenbooks.com/free1014380

ISBN 978-0-332-24417-4
PIBN 11014380

Year Book

of the

v York Southern
Society

For the Year 1914–15

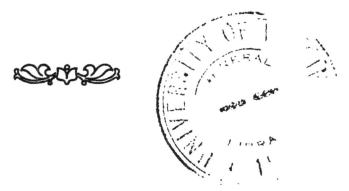

New York, 1914

5

CONTENTS

OFFICERS

1914 to 1915

President
W. W. FULLER

Vice-President
S. R. BERTRON

Treasurer
WILLIAM D. BUCKNER

Secretary
STEPHEN L. SNOWDEN

EXECUTIVE COMMITTEES

Class of 1914	*Class of* 1915
To serve until March, 1915.	To serve until March, 1916.
ARCHIBALD R. WATSON	GEORGE M. LAMONTE
JOHN P. EAST	JAMES C. MCREYNOLDS
ISAAC R. OELAND	WILLIAM A. BARBER
DR. ROBERT C. MYLES	PHELAN BEALE

Class of 1916
To serve until March, 1917

JOHN G. LONSDALE
ROBERT W. B. ELLIOTT
SAMUEL MCROBERTS
GEORGE B. COVINGTON

Chaplain
REV. ST. CLAIR HESTER, D.D.

SECRETARY'S OFFICE: 34 Pine Street,
Telephone No. 5832 John

5

STANDING COMMITTEES

1914 to 1915

Committee on Admissions

John P. East
    (Chairman)
George B. Covington
Robert W. B. Elliott

Auditing Committee

Phelan Beale
    (Chairman)
Jas. Lowry Dale
A. M. Carr

Entertainment Committee

J. Terry West
    (Chairman)
Theodore H. Price
Malcolm L. Meacham

Dinner Committee

John S. Primrose
    (Chairman)
Frank Trenholm
William Van Wyck

Committee on Speakers for Annual Dinner

Archibald R. Watson
    (Chairman)
J. Markham Marshall
John B. Cobb

Committee on Investment and Distribution of Charity Fund

Wm. D. Buckner
    (Chairman)
Dr. Fielding L. Taylor
Robert L. Harrison

Nominating Committee

Walter L. McCorkle
Robert Adamson
Stuart G. Gibboney
John P. East

Committee on Publication of Year Book

Stephen L. Snowden
    (Chairman)
Thomas S. Fuller
David N. Barrows

FORMER OFFICERS AND MEMBERS OF
EXECUTIVE COMMITTEES
From 1886 to 1914

Presidents

ALGERNON SYDNEY SULLIVAN
FRANCIS R. RIVES
JOHN C. CALHOUN
HUGH R. GARDEN
JAMES H. PARKER
ROBERT L. HARRISON
CHARLES A. DESHON

JOHN R. ABNEY
HUGH S. THOMPSON
DR. WILLIAM M. POLK
AUGUSTUS VAN WYCK
MARION J. VERDERY
DR. JOHN A. WYETH
WILLIAM G. McADOO

WALTER L. McCORKLE

Vice-Presidents

BURTON N. HARRISON
A. G. DICKINSON
JOHN C. CALHOUN
BALLARD SMITH
JOHN NEWTON
VIRGINIUS DABNEY
WILLIAM L. TRENHOLM
JAMES H. PARKER
EVAN THOMAS
WILLIAM P. ST. JOHN
ROBERT L. HARRISON
DR. JOHN A. WYETH
CHARLES A. DESHON

JAMES SWANN
CLARENCE CARY
JOHN H. INMAN
PETER MALLETT
WILLIAM P. THOMPSON
JOHN R. ABNEY
HUGH S. THOMPSON
DR. WILLIAM M. POLK
AUGUSTUS VAN WYCK
MARION J. VERDERY
HON. WILLIAM LINDSAY
WALTER L. McCORKLE
GEORGE GORDON BATTLE

Treasurers

WALTER L. McCORKLE
HOWARD SAUNDERS
JAMES L. JOHNSON
WILLIAM F. McCOMBS, JR.

HETH LORTON
GASTON HARDY
WILLIS BROWNING
JOHN P. EAST

WILLIAM D. BUCKNER

8

Lorenzo Semple
Peter Mallett
George Gordon Battle
John R. McKay
Thomas Marshall
James L. Johnson
Lindsay Russell
Charles Baskerville
William E. G. Gaillard
Lewis Nixon
E. Lowndes Rhett
George H. Sullivan
John A. Faust
Marion J. Verdery
Hugh S. Thompson

Percy S. Mallett
Hon. William Lindsay
William D. Buckner
J. Lynch Pendergast
Dr. George Bolling Lee
Thomas J. McGuire
Frank L. Polk
Hon. H. M. Somerville
S. R. Bertron
Francis G. Caffey
Gaston Hardy
Robert Adamson
Dr. Fielding L. Taylor
James S. Meng
George W. Neville

ENTERTAINMENTS

During the past year the Society held the following entertainments:

Entertainment and Smoker,
   Saturday, October 25, 1913, Waldorf-Astoria.
Entertainment for Charity,
   Thursday, November 13, 1913, Waldorf-Astoria.
Annual Dinner,
   Wednesday, December 10, 1913, Waldorf-Astoria.
Hearthstone Meeting,
   Monday, January 12, 1914, Waldorf-Astoria.
Dixie Dinner and Colonial Ball,
   Monday, February 23, 1914, Hotel Astor.
Annual Meeting and Smoker,
   Thursday, March 5, 1914, Waldorf-Astoria.

ENTERTAINMENTS SCHEDULED TO BE GIVEN DURING SEASON OF 1914–1915

Entertainment and Smoker,
   Saturday, October 24, 1914, Waldorf-Astoria.
Entertainment for Charity,
   Thursday, November 12, 1914,
Annual Dinner,
   Wednesday, December 9, 1914, Waldorf-Astoria.
Entertainment and Dance,
   Monday, January 11, 1915, Waldorf-Astoria.
Dixie Dinner and Colonial Ball,
   Tuesday, February 23, 1915, Hotel Astor.
Annual Meeting and Smoker,
   Thursday, March 4, 1915, Waldorf-Astoria.

TWENTY-EIGHTH ANNUAL DINNER OF THE NEW YORK SOUTHERN SOCIETY

HE Twenty-eighth Annual Dinner of the New York Southern Society was held in the Grand Ball Room of the Waldorf-Astoria, on Wednesday evening, December 10, 1913. Toasts were responded to by Dr. John Huston Finley, Commissioner of the Department of Education of the State of New York, Hon. John Purroy Mitchel, at that time Mayor-elect of the City of New York; Professor Raleigh C. Minor, of the University of Virginia, and Hon. Dudley Field Malone, Collector of the Port of New York.

T the conclusion of the dinner, Mr. Walter L. McCorkle, the President of the Society, and who presided at the dinner as Toastmaster, addressed the Society as follows:

Fellow Members of the Society, Ladies and Gentlemen:

It is with satisfaction and pride that I greet you again upon our annual reunion, and on behalf of the Society, I extend to you welcome. I offer you that hospitality which has characterized the dinners of this Society since its organization.

We welcome most heartily the gentlemen who have kindly consented to address us, the representatives of the Army and Navy, and especially those representatives of our sister societies who always do us the honor of coming to us with their best wishes and generous interest.

To you, Ladies, who are the flowers of this occasion, to you who give inspiration to the speakers by the charm of your gracious presence, we offer that homage which is due you and ask you to accept our assurance that we entertain an admiration for you which we recognize we "can ne'er express yet cannot at all conceal."

Of our society, I beg to report a pursuance, during the past year, of the even tenor of its way, and that even tenor has been of the flourishing variety.

Its membership is greater than at any previous time.

It has not been difficult for us to increase our numbers, but it has been very difficult to improve the quality. However, your Committee on Admissions exercises great care to maintain the standard.

The treasury is in a most healthful condition. Under the fostering care of our faithful Treasurer it continues to expand, regardless of the efforts of the Committee on Charity to find Southerners in this community who are willing to come forward and help themselves to it.

We are compelled to record the loss by death during the past year of twelve members of the Society. The mention of their names will ensure your endorsement of their thorough worth.

Who here does not pay willing tribute to the memory of such men as Thomas J. McGuire, Dr. Prince A. Morrow, James A. Moffett, Judge William A. Keener, J. Shepherd Clark, Dr. Frank Hartley, and Jennings S. Cox,—all men of dignified achievement, whose sturdy integrity and kindly nature made them an honor to any organization to which they belonged. We deeply deplore their loss.

In the fret and fever of our intense metropolitan life, to one thing your organization has been faithful. We have met annually now for almost thirty years to take a grateful, reverent look backward, to keep alive our altar fires, and to recall the virtues of those from whom we have descended.

Few experiences more than occasions of this character, where men of different sections, of different tastes, of different interests, touch elbows and give good cheer to each other, have a wider influence in the formation of public opinion—the kind of public opinion that has sentiment under and behind it.   These gatherings count for more than either the platform, the rostrum, or the stump, and I might almost say the pulpit itself, in making public opinion.

Of the homeland we can say that she is awake alike in mind and energy, and is going forward not backward. She is growing in prosperity and in practical Americanism.

At that recent notable meeting of representative citizens of this Republic held in Mobile, where every section of the South was represented, in that wonderful address by the President of the United States and in speeches made by members of the Cabinet and other distinguished representatives present, every utterance breathed wise counsel and inspiring prophecies of the increasing greatness of the South.

Some momentous things have occurred, since we met together last December. Conspicuous among these is the foremost fact that for the first time in more than half a century a Southern-born man is the Chief Executive of this government; over this we have a right to felicitate ourselves.   Besides this many members of this Society have, to our regret, changed their address to Washington City and various other parts of the civilized world through political preferment.

14

In fact, as we recall McReynolds, McAdoo, Dr. Walter Page and Thomas Nelson Page, the genial Joe Willard, Col. Francis G. Caffey, Snowden Marshall, and Walker Vick, we feel that when the President stated to us in this room one year ago that he saw men in his audience who were going to help him to interpret the general wisdom of the country, he certainly has kept his word.

In the exercise of wisdom and patience, in dealing with the great problems that confront every Executive of this country, we are confident that President Wilson is measuring up to the highest expectations of his friends. In the accomplishment of great work he has had but few equals in the high office he holds, and in his earnest desire to maintain the peace of the republic there are none but who must say he has exercised all the great powers of statesmanship with which he is endowed.

His assertion that the United States will never wage a war for conquest is in thorough keeping with the patriotic view that has ever characterized an illustrious line of his predecessors.

The United States has never waged a war of conquest. The motive which actuated our revolutionary fathers was not for possession, but for liberty. All our other wars have been for the preservation of the nation and the maintenance of our inheritance. That with Spain was in no way in our interest but for the liberty of the oppressed, the relief of the suffering, and the freedom

15

of those that were bound. The glory of this nation in pursuing that policy has been as remarkable as her founding and her peace.

We feel well assured that President Wilson is working with one desire only; that of serving the American people with the best of his ability, and he will proceed on those lines that make for the continued peace and prosperity of this Republic.

Those who now say they don't understand certain of his policies will understand them better next year. I am sure later on they will realize that the President has done something big; that he has done it in a way to give the United States a new claim to honor among the nations of the earth.

Such a spirit as he possesses will wear out the longest tyranny and assist at the coronation of a brighter destiny.

Your Dinner Committee has offered you an attractive menu card depicting some of the events that transpired almost a century and a half since, and as we hark back, we can truly say that there is no other country in the world that points to such glorious achievements on land and sea, such traditions, history, literature and devotion to ideals as does ours.

The devotion of the Colonists to each other in those trying days has not been excelled in the history of the world. When the dark days came, New England, New York, and Virginia locked arms in standing for the rights of Englishmen against the tyranny of Englishmen. And

when the clouds of war were gone, New England gave to
us men with high ideals of life and patriotism, and Virginia furnished men who proved themselves masters in
constitutional government.

The Scotch Irishmen under Mr. Jefferson made the
Valley of Virginia the fountain of American Democracy
as New England had made her stony soil the nursery of
free institutions.

The names of the Massachusetts patriots of the
Revolution are inseparably connected with those of
Washington, Jefferson, Marshall, and Madison. It was
John Adams who, when the second Constitutional Con-
gress was considering the appointment of a Commander-
in-Chief to go to Cambridge and take command of the
Colonial troops, urged the appointment not of a Massa-
chusetts man but of Col. George Washington.

On the very day when the Battle of Bunker Hill was
fought, Adams wrote home, "I can now inform you that
Congress has made choice of the modest and virtuous,
the generous, amiable, and brave George Washington,
Esq., to be General of the American Army, that he is to
repair as soon as possible to the camp before Boston.
This appointment will have a great effect in cementing
and securing the union of these Colonies."

And to-day as their successors, and in some measure
I trust their representatives, we are ready to give voice
to the sentiment that there are no two peoples in the
world who quietly enjoy so much each other's admiration

and commendation, or wince so smartly under each other's disapproval.

This evening for the first time in many years, we rejoice to say that our elder sister, The New England Society, has sent to us their representative. No man can fail to rejoice in the complete unity of our land, in the perpetual unity of this great nation, and I desire to emphasize this to our brother of New England. This is the *sentiment* of a nation in whose veins courses the blood of soldiers, and the blood of women worthy to be the mothers of a race of soldiers.

I renew my congratulations to you, Gentlemen, upon the prosperous condition of the Society and upon the advanced position which it has won—that of especially standing in all things for what is best, for the preservation of the good name of the great metropolis, where we have made our home, and for the largest measure of good will between the land of our birth and that of every other portion of our Country.

This is probably the last annual banquet of the Southern Society at which I shall have the honor of presiding. In closing my official term, I desire to leave this thought with you—the gospel of fellowship and patriotism is the foundation of all useful citizenship, and I pray that this organization may always do its part in furthering the great cause for which all true Americans stand—namely, the perpetuation of human liberty under a constitutional form of government.

I invite you to rise and toast with me the glory of the Republic and drink to the health and happiness of the President of the United States.

(The toast was drunk standing.)

HE TOASTMASTER: Gentlemen, we are to-night, as is usual on these occasions, honored by the presence of the goddesses of grace and beauty. Following the chivalrous custom of our fathers we accord them first honor.

I invite you to join in a health to those whose smile is a gracious benediction and in the light of whose eyes we would live forever. (Rising toast to the ladies.)

The first toast of the evening is "The City of New York," the city that has not only captured but has adopted us. I regret very much to state that our worthy Mayor, Hon. Ardolph R. Kline, who had accepted our invitation to respond to this toast is ill and unable to be present.

Learning is the lamp by which all the peoples of the earth must march in fulfillment of the highest glory of human destiny.

I have the honor to present to you Dr. John Huston Finley who holds aloft the torch of learning for the guidance of the people of this Empire State.

DR. JOHN HUSTON FINLEY: Being called upon unexpectedly to speak at this moment, I think I owe it to the sources of inspiration to which reference has just been made by your President, that is, to the Goddesses,

20

to say that I have not had time to take advantage of this inspiration which sits above us.

Your President was able to anticipate that inspiration. He was able to make most eloquent reference to it. But not having attended a Southern Society dinner for a long time, I could not have anticipated such an *inspiration*, and so, of course, I am neither prepared for it, nor can I immediately take advantage of it. If I could have an hour in which to sit undisturbed by the speeches of others in the presence of that inspiration and it were not too intense in any one particular direction, I should be able to make a speech that would be worthy of this occasion.

Some one asked me, as I approached the door (and I failed to get into the procession), how it was that one of my birth and homeliness of countenance could expect to gain admission to a Southern Society dinner: "Well," I said, "I had a mother who had the same name as the grandmother of the chairman of the National Democratic Committee, and he was born in Arkansas." And I have since thought of another reason. This is the reason.

I once had my collar-bone broken by that handsome giant, Herbert Noble, who comes from the state of Maryland. I came into this world, that is I was born, in the North, but my skeleton, as a result of an encounter with Herbert Noble on the football field, was repaired in the South.

I do not like to begin by making excuses; but that personification of honor and bravery, General John B. Gordon tells this incident in his reminiscences, which is very pertinent to my feelings to-night. That is, I anticipated it would be pertinent to my feelings, and so I had it in mind.

The story is of an incident in a battle which one or both of us wish to forget. I have forgotten, on just which side it occurred, but the guns of one side had been making great gaps through the lines of the other side (I thought it was the Southern side that had been making the gaps through the Northern lines, but I don't know how General Gordon could have known about it if that were the case). Through one of these gaps, a rabbit was seen to be flying to the rear, displaying a white flag of truce, and an Irish man seeing it said, "Go it, Molly Cottontail, I wish I were going where you are going, and I would be going, too, if it were not for my car-akter (character)" and I wish to say that except for my car-akter (my character) that is to say, except for my promise to Mr. Battle I would take to my heels in the presence of this array, which is more terrifying, if you will believe me, with all its charm and cordiality than an army with banners.

When I looked over the list of speakers, the "Honorable" list of speakers (I noticed that they were all "honorable" men, except one), and I anticipated that everything that could be truthfully and eloquently said in this latitude concerning the South, would have been

said, or would be about to be said, and so I decided not
to enter that competitive field held by the Irish and the
Southerners.

With my inherited Scotch thrift, I decided to make
my small rhetorical investment in another field, in lines
that run transversely to those lines which embrace that
territory that is dearest to you. I am going to speak for
a moment about the lines of longitude.

When we first became conscious of the sphericity
of the earth, we found it covered with a network of lines.
We were told by the geography that these lines were
imaginary lines. And we were obliged by the teacher
to so state; and when we came out into the world, we
found that they were invisible, at any rate.

I can remember how, even in my years of maturity,
that when I was going down into the Caribbean Sea,
I was disappointed to find that there was no visible
indication of the Tropic of Cancer. Is it the Tropic of
Cancer or Capricorn? It is the one on this side. But
we have learned that those lines, though they were
called imaginary by the geography and by the teacher,
were very real lines. We know, for example, that the
sun always turns about, that it is prevented from coming farther north by this imaginary line, this Tropic of
Cancer shall we say? And we know when the sun goes
to the other side of the Equator, there is another line
there, which just a little before Christmas will stop the
sun and make it come back. If it didn't do that, Mr.

23

Coffin here, before me, the head of the General Electric, would have a monopoly of light—not that I would object to that. The absent speaker at first announced to speak here to-night probably would.

These lines of latitude are indeed very real lines. Men have been willing to die for lines of latitude. I sat with an Oregon man at luncheon to-day, and he reminded me of that battle-cry for a line of latitude ("Fifty-four, forty, or fight".) And there are certain other lines of latitude which we might but shall not mention to-night. But for a line of longitude, so far as I can remember at the moment, no one has been willing to die, except the Aborigines and I fancy they did not know what they were dying for.

Hon. Timothy Healy once said no one would die for the Meridian of Greenwich. As you remember the Meridian of Greenwich is the source of all longitude. And I recall, my memory being recently refreshed, that Mr. Chesterton in commenting upon that statement, said it was because Greenwich does not "cohere" in the sense in which Athens or Sparta cohered, or I think we might add, those nationalities which have followed the lines of latitude around the earth; and yet I am thinking, and this is about all I am going to say, that we are approaching the era of the line of longitude. I suppose even now, men would not die for the Meridian of Greenwich, but I am not sure that men would not die for, let us say— well, I have forgotten what that line of longitude is that

24

passes just the other side of the point of South America. I am not sure that men would not die for that parallel of longitude. You might call it, perhaps, the "Tropic of Monroe."

Possibly there will be another tropic in the Pacific some day. I don't know what name we shall give to it. My point is this: we have followed lines of latitude. We have followed the Isotherms. (Col. Harrison, at my side, knows what Isotherms are, but some of the rest of you may not.) He is on the School Board, so of course he knows. They are lines of like temperature. But now we carry our climates with us and our accustomed foods. We carry refrigerators to the Equator and we carry pemmican to the poles. We have no Frigid Zones; we have no Torrid Zones, in a sense. We are coming to the time of hemispherical and longitudinal development—of closer relations between North and South, in the United States and in America.

I know, perhaps, this is not just the right thing to say at this dinner, which celebrates a latitude.

But whether this expression of my theory be entirely acceptable or not, I do believe that this North and South, this hemispherical development is desirable. Otherwise we are likely to be stratified permanently. If you will let me change the figure, the warp has been laid across this continent by civilization, and the problem is to carry the transverse threads, the woof, through these patches of gray, or of black, or of white, or green, or red, or whatever they may be, that we may have a lasting and non-tearable fabric, penetrated by new world purposes and hopes that will present to the world a design of beauty, more glorious than the world has ever known in the past.

I was last night, as some of you know, at a dinner of the Champlain Association. Mingling here to-night with you who come from a lower latitude, I feel that I am myself a personification of a line of longitude. I know I am not as attractive to those who sit about and above as those other lines which lie wholly within the Southern zone, but I am grateful to the Almighty now that my embarrassment is over, I am grateful that I have been permitted to have this experience of connecting the land of the snows with the land of the orange trees, without reducing the temperature to the freezing point, and that I have been permitted to say this word in prophecy of the coming of the time when we shall all be as ready to give our devotion to the parallels of longitude as we have been to give it to parallels of latitude.

HE TOASTMASTER: Gentlemen, this city of our choice has a close place in our affection and we are to her loyal. We are most fortunate this evening in having with us a grandson of old Virginia, who has been called recently to the high office of Chief Executive of this great municipality. I have the honor to introduce to you, Hon. John Purroy Mitchel, Mayor-elect of the city of New York.

HON. JOHN PURROY MITCHEL: Mr. President, and Ladies and Gentlemen of the Southern Society: I am grateful to your committee for the invitation to come here this evening. I received it shortly before I left the city for the vacation which was necessary after the labors of the campaign, and at a time when I was not certain whether it would be possible, conveniently, to make arrangements, to meet the engagement of this dinner, but when Mr. Adamson told me that the Southern Society wanted me to attend this dinner, I told him that I would so arrange my affairs as to bring about my return to the city in time to come to this dinner, for it was one that I would not miss.

Your President referred to me as a grandson of old Virginia, wasn't it?

THE TOASTMASTER: Quite right, Sir.

MAYOR MITCHEL (Continuing): For no other

27

reason than because the members of this Society, or some
of them, at least, voted for me in the recent election,
but perhaps I have a somewhat better claim to the title
than that, in view of the fact that my grandfather, while
not born in Virginia, was a resident of the State at the
opening of the War, and enlisted in the service of the
Confederacy, together with his three sons, my father and
my two uncles.

In fact, gentlemen, at the time when I was chosen to
represent the Fusion forces in the recent campaign, one of
the newspapers, commenting upon the choice and point-
ing out the many excellent reasons why my candidacy
was the weakest that could have been selected, referred to
the fact as a reason for that, that all of my grandfather's
family had given their services to the Confederacy; that
my father had enlisted with the first regiment that went
out of Virginia, and that two of my uncles had given
their lives in the service of that Cause, and thought that
that was a reason why the citizenship of New York
would not consider me a proper chief executive for the
city.

Well, I take the word of your President that the
members of this Society, at least, did not find in those
facts a good reason for rejecting my candidacy.   Nor do
I believe that in this era and at this time, the citizenship
of this city or of any city of this country or of any part
of this country would find in those facts, or in any
similar facts, a reason for voting either against or for

any particular candidate for public office, and that is as it should be.

I do feel that I have to acknowledge a personal debt of gratitude to the many southern citizens of this city, of the citizens of this city of southern birth, because I know that I had nowhere in my candidacy for the Mayoralty a more hearty support than among the southern democrats of New York who felt with me that the truest democracy is that which finds its expression primarily in the service of the people, rather than in the service of any small group of men who choose to call themselves their representatives.

Now, in the invitations which have come to me to speak at public dinners, during the few days that intervene between the present time and the first of January, grateful and pleasant as those invitations are, I find a certain embarrassment, because it is really difficult to find anything to say that will be of interest to my hearers.

You do not want to hear from me a discussion of the plans and the program of the new city administration. Those were discussed amply during the campaign. We told you then what we proposed to do, if you elected us to office, and the time for reviewing and re-stating that program and those promises is not now before we have begun fulfillment. I think the time for discussing them is when we are actively engaged in the fulfillment, and when we may discuss with you directly whether or not we are living up to the promises that we made you during

29

the campaign. And I prefer, therefore, as far as possible, to postpone those discussions until we have actively launched forth into the work of the new administration, and then I hope to discuss them fully and intimately and openly with the people of this city.

The other subject which would be of interest to you, and which I know is of burning interest to the representatives of the press, because that has been made very apparent to me during the past two or three days, is the matter of appointments to the departments of the city government, but for obvious reasons, gentlemen, that subject is not open to me yet. It will doubtless be discussed very fully by you after my announcements are made.

There is, however, one subject to which I would like to make brief allusion here to-night, because this is the first dinner at which I have felt that the subject was open to me. I have noticed, although I was not able to read the papers very much during my absence from the city, but I have noticed in the few advices that reached me, that there has been here a good deal of discussion concerning plans for—shall I call it reorganization of the local Democratic Party, or for the upbuilding of a more genuinely democratic party in this city. I have seen those plans alluded to, and I have noticed that speculation has been indulged in as to whether the newly elected Mayor would take an active part, as Mayor, in that undertaking.

While perhaps it, is unnecessary to repeat now what I said so often during the campaign, and I mean what I say during campaigns as well afterwards as at the time, still I will say this again and now. As a Democrat, but more especially as a citizen of New York, I am interested in seeing here a representative, a creditable Democratic Party in which we can all take a pride.

As a Democrat, as a citizen of this city, as an individual, I never proposed to surrender my right to take part as an individual in any political movement of which I approve, but, my friends, I say to you that as Mayor of New York I am pledged by every utterance during the campaign in no way to lend the power, the prestige, or the opportunities of that office to the upbuilding of any party, of any faction, or any group.

No man will be appointed by me to office simply because he belonged to one of the parties which endorsed my candidacy at its primary. No man will be appointed by me to office whose purpose is to use that office, directly or indirectly, for the upbuilding of any particular party in this city, and no man will be retained by me in office who develops such a purpose after appointment, although I have no expectation of any such development.

I simply say this to you in order that this speculation may be ended now, and this discussion may proceed no further, and I repeat that this administration of the city government is to be non-partisan.

We were elected not to do the work of a particular

31

party. We were elected not as candidates in State and National elections are selected, where they may logically consider that they have become the leaders of the parties that elected them, but we were elected by the citizenship of New York to give a business administration of its affairs, without consideration of politics, and that, in so far as I have ability and power, I propose to do.

Your President on one or two occasions has been good enough to suggest to me that I have title to membership in this Society. For one reason or another, chiefly because I have been more or less pressed for time, and have overlooked the matter, I have never yet taken advantage of his very kind offer to help me to become a member of the Southern Society, but now that the customary and time-honored period for joining new organizations,—namely, the campaign—has passed, I may say to you that I am going to take advantage of your President's offer, and that I hope when I meet the members of this Society again, that I will meet them as one.

HE TOASTMASTER: Our next speaker, a son of the Sacred Soil, as John Randolph ever referred to the "Old Dominion," comes to us fresh from the halls of the University. He has kindly consented to speak to you of some Political Problems.

It is with more than ordinary pleasure I introduce to you Prof. Raleigh C. Minor, of the University of Virginia.

PROFESSOR RALEIGH C. MINOR: Mr. Toastmaster and members of the Southern Society, Ladies and Gentlemen: I shall take this opportunity to express to you my grateful appreciation of the many kindnesses and courtesies that have been extended to me during my brief visit.

The subject I have chosen is a very complex one, and for that reason, I wish to adhere very closely to my manuscript. With that as guide and monitor, I will not detain you long.

Whither are we drifting? Toward tumultuous seas or safe and quiet harborage?

None can doubt that a deep-seated unrest pervades the American people. It shows itself in many ways: amongst others in a demand for political reforms, which allure us with golden promises of a regeneration that shall free us not only from the shackles of an "invisible government," but from the manacles of convention and custom.

Myriads of voices are clamoring for this or that change in our habits of life and thought, nay, in our most cherished convictions,—until, bewildered by the clash and din, we are tempted to stand, stupidly staring at the problems of life, without trying to solve them.

Out of this Babel comes a still, small voice whispering insistently to those who will hear that they cling to the old landmarks; that human nature has not altered materially with the passing of the centuries; that ambition, avarice, selfishness, and all the painful family of woe to the weak and defenseless are yet with us; and that we be cautious in exchanging the old convictions of mankind, fortified by ages of human experience, for new and untried theories, however splendid they may seem to the vision of the dreamer.

From the standpoint of government the most remarkable of these present-day movements is that looking to the complete and direct control of government in all its departments by the people, reckoned by numerical majorities, not by the weight of sound public opinion.

The *legislative* action of government is to be subjected to this direct control through the initiative and referendum; its executive action through the recall; and its judicial action through the recall of judges or of judicial decisions.

Whatever the means used, the final result is to be

determined by numerical majorities of the voters who, through the powers thus conferred, will be enabled to disregard all the constitutional checks and balances for the protection of the minority that have so painfully been built up from the materials furnished by the history and experience of mankind.

This is in effect revolution.   In the last analysis it is a change from constitutional government to arbitrary despotism,—the despotism of a numerical majority of the people, which may be as oppressive and tyrannical as any other.

In the States where these principles have been fully established, the Federal Constitution is the only ultimate safeguard against such tyranny and oppression.

Nor are indications wanting that attempts will be made to storm even that citadel of constitutional rights, so that the same principles may be applied in the administration of the Federal government.   Indeed the first step in that direction is at this moment being taken.

A sub-committee of the Senate Judiciary Committee has favorably reported a proposal to alter the mode of amending the Constitution.   The resolution as reported, is in the following words:

"Whenever the legislatures of sixteen States shall adopt resolutions proposing any amendment, and the same are certified to the President of the United States, or whenever fifteen per centum of the voters in twenty-four States present to the President petitions, authenticated by the respective governors of the said States, proposing any amendment, the President shall submit the same to the several States, and in either case any such amendment shall be valid to all intents and purposes as a part of the Constitution when ratified by two thirds of the several States, acting either by direct vote of the people or by the legislatures, as may be determined by State law. *Provided*, that no State, without its consent, shall be deprived of its equal suffrage in the Senate."

This proposal would introduce the principles of the initiative and referendum into the Federal Constitution at its most vital point.

If there were time, it might be easily shown, I think, that these revolutionary conceptions owe their origin mainly to the inefficiency of the States in their executive administration, and their lack of responsiveness to popular opinion,—particularly in the legislative and judicial departments.

It is a curious fact that the inefficiency of State administration is due in large measure to the very same departure from the principles of representative government that is now urged as the remedy. Our political doctors are seeking to enforce the old adage that the hair of the dog is good for the bite.

In the effort to give the people more direct control, the States have decentralized themselves and, confusing local self-government with central authority, have provided that governmental functions pertaining to the whole State shall be exercised by officials locally elected and therefore responsible only to their local constituents, not to the State at large nor to its central government.

The typical State constitution, while solemnly proclaiming that the Governor is the chief executive, and, as such, shall see that the laws be faithfully executed, has taken pains to deny him, for the most part, the power of appointment and removal, and generally to deprive him of all real executive powers, save those of the veto, the pardon, the command of the militia, and a few of lesser moment.

Thus, the whole field of State revenue is intrusted to officers locally elected, who, for political reasons, are much more inclined to let their constituents off with a minimum of taxation than to give the State a square deal.   In Virginia, for instance, of one hundred counties, seventy-one receive more this year from the State treasury than they pay into it.   Were these officials appointed and removable by the Governor, who can doubt that the results would be far different?

So it is with the State departments of Justice.   The prosecuting attorneys are usually elected by the people in each city and county.   There is no central authority having power to appoint, to remove, or to substitute one of these officials for another in a particular case, or to collect the whole force of the State in the prosecution of a powerful or influential criminal.

In the matters of the preservation of public order,

the enforcement of legal process, the making and repair of highways, the preservation of the public health, the care of the indigent or afflicted, the supervision of jails and prisons, and so on, the story is the same.   There is no centralization of authority.   Each local officer does what seems good in his own sight, responsible to none but the local constituents who elect him, and anxious to find favor only with them.

From such soil and with such tillage what can be reaped but a harvest of inefficiency?   No single State has followed the example set by the Federal Constitution in creating a strong executive, with full powers of appointment and removal and with full accountability for the due administration of the laws.

Perhaps no plan could be devised better adapted to destroy or conceal all official responsibility for maladministration than that which has thus been habitually followed by the States.   Is it to be wondered at that the people, conscious of the inefficiency, but ignorant where to lay the blame, either turn to the efficient general government for relief, or seek, through the recall or otherwise, to fix a responsibility which does not now exist?

The States have departed from the principles of representative government, substituting in its place a sort of localized democracy.   I submit that the proper remedy is not more democracy, in the form of the recall, but a return to the true principles of representation which demand the wedding of responsibility to power.   Give the chief executive the power needful to make him such in reality as well as in name; make him the full and complete political head of the State, as the President is of the United States; and then hold him to strict account for the administration of public affairs.

But the clamor for the initiative, referendum, and recall is perhaps due more to lack of responsiveness to public opinion on the part of the legislative and judicial departments of the States than to the inefficiency of the executive department.

The failure of the State legislatures in this regard has been quite generally ascribed to the corrupt influence of special interests. That the assumption is in some instances true will hardly be denied.

But a more pervasive cause is to be found in the ignorance and want of training of the legislators. Neither the senators nor the members of the lower house are supposed to represent particular and special interests, but only the general interests of all their constituents.

If each legislator were an adept in all trades, occupations and professions and an expert in all arts and sciences, the theory might work well. But this cannot be expected even of legislators. On the contrary, many of them are inexperienced or untrained. At best they can only be adepts in some particular art, business, or science.

It is not necessary then to assume legislative corruption in order to explain why much of our legislation is inefficient or even actually vicious, injurious, and unjust. Ignorance of the details of the subjects dealt with is enough to insure it.

John C. Calhoun, in his remarkable "Discourse on Government" has pointed out a political principle which, while taken advantage of in the Federal Constitution, has not been fully utilized by the States. I refer to his doctrine of *concurrent majorities*.

This doctrine, upon which are based all constitutional checks and balances, saves society from despotism whether the despot be an absolute monarch, an oligarchy, or a numerical majority of the people.

The principle may be expressed in the form that the great interests of the State shall each have a concurrent voice in, or else a veto upon, governmental action.

In the operation of the United States government, this is exemplified by the fact that each house of Congress has a veto upon the other; that the executive has a qualified veto upon the action of Congress, and to a limited extent upon the courts, through the pardoning power and the occasional need of its aid to enforce their judgments; and that the courts possess a like limited veto power upon legislative action through their power to declare laws unconstitutional, and upon executive action through their power to hold subordinate executive officials liable for damage caused by their unlawful acts. To this extent the States also have utilized the doctrine.

But in one important respect the States have failed

40

to follow the lead of the Federal Constitution in enforcing the principle.

In the Federal convention of 1789, two great interests contended for mastery. The first was population; the other the equal sovereignty of the States. Many believed that the preponderating influence in the general government should rest with the people numerically considered. Others believed it should rest with the States as sovereigns, each State having an equal voice, regardless of population. Neither party was willing to yield, so that it became one of the gravest problems of the convention to reconcile these discordant views.

It was finally accomplished through the application of this principle of concurrent majorities. The Senate was made to represent the equal sovereignty of the States, the House of Representatives the numerical majorities of the people. Each of these great interests thus possess a veto upon the action of the other; and both must concur before any legislative action may be taken.

The States, however, have not seen fit to make such a use of this principle in the organization of their legislative departments. Instead of choosing great and important interests and balancing them against the numerical majorities of the people, they have contented themselves with balancing the numerical majority in one district against that in another. Thus, the whole machinery of State government in the final analysis rests in the hands of mere popular majorities.

The members of the lower house of a State legislature are elected by numerical majorities of the voters resident in certain districts; the senators are elected by like majorities, but in larger districts; the Governor and certain other executive officials are elected by a majority of the people of the entire State; subordinate executive officials by majorities in smaller election districts; and in most of the States even the judges are elected by popular majorities in larger or smaller districts.

It is at this point that the States have neglected the salutary principle of concurrent majorities, and this neglect, I contend, is in large measure responsible for the initiative and referendum.

Within each commonwealth are great interests constantly clamoring for or against legislation. They can officially voice their views in the legislative halls only through the representatives elected from their respective districts. But the representative is elected not to represent them specially, but the whole constituency. He may even have been elected upon a platform openly hostile to them. If he is corrupt, and these interests are rich and powerful, he probably makes a secret bargain with them. If he is honest, and the legislation complex, he is seldom in a position to know or to learn what is really for the welfare of his constituents as a whole. In his bewilderment, his final attitude is as apt to be the work of chance as of conviction.

Is it not possible to exchange for such haphazard

legislation a more scientific system?   Why not seek out
those overshadowing interests in each state, which,
taken collectively, would embrace practically all the
voters, and make these the basis of representation in the
State Senates, leaving the lower house to represent, as
now, the people reckoned by numbers merely?

For example, suppose that the great interests thus
chosen are five, agriculture, commerce, manufacture,
education, and labor; that each of these be entitled to
such representation in the State Senates as its importance
and the number of persons attached to the particular
interest may demand; and that each voter in the State
be permitted to align himself with one or the other of
these interests in the election of senators.

Would it not result that each of these great interests,
instead of being represented or misrepresented, as the
case may be, by persons, more or less ignorant of its
needs, might find a voice through its own chosen representatives?

Should there be log-rolling between the interests to
secure legislation, we might at least be sure that it would
be more open and notorious than now, and that the laws
enacted would not be more hurtful to the majority of the
people since they must also pass the lower house repre-
senting the numerical majority.   Such log-rolling could
never be worse than the secret lobbying and corruption,
or the ignorance and misinformation that now animates
legislation.

The plan would tend to transfer the scene of the real legislative battles from the dark and secret recesses of the legislator's closet into the clearer light of the Senate Hall; and the legislation thus enacted, resting upon a broader basis, would voice a sounder and safer public opinion. The people would be equally represented in each house, but in different aspects or from different angles.

Finally, dissatisfaction with the decisions and procedure of the *courts*, has been responsible for the development of the two new political dogmas,—the recall of the judges and the recall of judicial decisions.

The recall of an executive officer is susceptible of some sort of logical defense. At worst, if subject to the recall, he is in the same position he would occupy were he elected for a short term and desired re-election.

Again, executive and legislative officials are generally expected, within constitutional limits, to carry out the desires of their constituents, though those desires be unwise. They represent the will,—even the capricious will,—of the people. Their failure to execute that will might, in some instances, be logically followed by popular vengeance.

But with the judges it is otherwise. They do not, or should not, represent the will, but the sober judgment of the people. So far from being subject to the passions or fickle caprice of the multitude, they ought to be as far removed therefrom as possible. This does not imply that judges should be insensible of a sound and well-digested public sentiment; but it does exclude sensitiveness to every breath of public clamor.

Let it be admitted that occasionally judges have tended to construe too strictly the constitutional limitations upon legislative powers, and have declared laws unconstitutional that should have been sustained. Let it be admitted that occasionally judges have been corrupt, or, with incompetence almost as criminal as corruption, have decided points contrary to law and popular rights. Let it be admitted that court procedure is antiquated, exasperatingly slow, and abounding in technicalities that might easily give place to more enlightened views of the administration of justice. The fact still remains that the recall, as a remedy, is worse than the disease, its tendency being to make *all* courts as corrupt or as partisan as the few have heretofore been, but in the opposite direction,—in favor of the popular will, though it conflicts with the legal rights and liberties of the private litigant.

If there be corruption, or incompetent disregard of public or private rights, on the part of some judges in some of the States, ought we not to reflect that this evil too may have its roots in the fact that we already have too much democracy in our State constitutions; and that instead of applying the remedy of more democracy, in the form of the recall, another and a better remedy might be to recall our past decision that judges be elected

by the people, and return to the conviction once preva-
lent that they should be appointed by a central authority.

But, after all, someone may say, these suggestions
touch only the surface of the trouble. The real source
of these revolutionary theories is the existence of the
irresponsible political boss and the corrupt alliance in
popular belief made between him and the interests. The
initiative, referendum, and recall are really weapons devised to wage a holy war against him and his allies.

Admitting this, it must be remembered that the boss
is the creature of modern democratic conditions. He
cannot thrive without an abundance of offices to divide
amongst his followers, and this aid and comfort he would
in most cases lose, did we return to the true principles of
representative government and fill the offices through
appointment by the central authority rather than
through election by local constituencies.

Most of the political evils that have caused the
demand for these radical departures from the theory of
real representative government are due to the initial
departures of our State constitutions from that theory,
in the vain attempt to give the people a part in government for which they are not fitted, throwing upon them
responsibilities they should never have been asked to
assume. The framers of the Federal Constitution made
no such mistake.

That ultimate and final control of government
should rest with the people is a fundamental postulate of

the representative theory. The chief executive and the legislative body must be directly responsible to them. But it would seem equally true that a grave error was made when the States extended the principle of direct control, through the suffrage, to the judiciary and to executive officers inferior to the governor.

It is the incapacity of the people to select properly this multitude of officials, and the resulting confusion and indifference of the voter, that is the chief cause of State inefficiency. It is this that has given to the political boss his opportunity.

If, then, too large a dose of democracy is the original cause of these disorders, it is surely not too radical an assumption that the remedy lies in diminishing rather than increasing the dose in future. Poison, if taken in large quantities, is sometimes less dangerous than if taken in smaller doses, because it acts as its own emetic, but there is no basis for the belief that democracy shares with it this valuable quality.

HE TOASTMASTER: As patriotic citizens, we are all deeply interested in the successful administration of the affairs of our National Government. When the President honored us with his presence one year ago, he stated that he saw men in his audience who were going to stand at his side and help him in the performance of the serious work before him.

We are honored to-night by the presence of one who was of that audience and who has been chosen to one of the most important positions under the administration.

I desire to present to you, Hon. Dudley Field Malone, Collector of the Port of New York.

HON. DUDLEY FIELD MALONE: Mr. President, Ladies and Gentlemen: I am in a very embarrassing position because it has been said the best was saved for the last. The best of what, I know not, since all of the subjects have been so thoroughly rehearsed in these brilliant, extemporaneous, and thoroughly prepared speeches.

Dr. Finley came here and spoke as a bird would warble on the limb of a Spring-like tree, with a speech that doubtless he had been working on for the last ten days.

Then John Mitchel came along with this story of

his about the vacation that precluded any attention to the invitation of the Southern Society, which he inadvertently admitted he received before he started and failed at all to inform us of the time that he spent when he was not shooting tigers in Panama, on the preparation of this speech.

And then the illustrious jurist from the University of Virginia came here and delivered his extemporaneous effort.

And, now, I am to come forth and deliver a thoroughly prepared speech about which I have given no thought until this evening.

Ladies, I am embarrassed at your presence, because John Mitchel will tell you that the office which I hold is in bad taste with the ladies.

However, if I may be personal with respect to the duties of my new position, I would say that the law which has caused such a great unpopularity toward me was put on the statute books before I came into office, and enforced with its present vigor by my immediate predecessor, Mayor Mitchel.

Moreover, I owe him this, because I have been telling all our mutual friends that his job was left me clean, and his desk was clear of hang-over duties. It is not so. I find that he has dodged one very embarrassing situation, namely, the protest of the militant and the peaceful suffragettes against their inability to get passes to go on the revenue cutters and climb up the sides of the steamships; and next week, I, with the calm complacency of an older man, must sit impassive to the guile and the joy and the charming influence of the ladies, who are going to prove to me that he was wrong, and that I must be right.

And so there are many embarrassments, but not the least is the thought that the delightful professor on my left is sincerely fearful of a growth of democracy in America.   He has not lived in the city of New York, or he would pray to God for a growth of real democracy.

He has not lived under the conditions under which we have lived, or he would be willing to realize, as he can with his genius, that there are tendencies due to new methods, which may be dangerous, but not nearly as dangerous when taken in hand by all the people who have a right to make their own mistakes, as when arrogated by a few, who have usurped authority, and who have no right to make our mistakes for us.

And so I also may be revolutionary.

John Mitchel is a non-partisan Mayor of New York. I am a non-partisan Collector of New York, but in my evenings there is nothing non-partisan about my political activities.

I am not interested in any reform, as I have said before, which merely contemplates one campaign, because the gentlemen with whom we intend to battle (not in a personal way, because there is nothing personal in our attitude, but for the purification of the party, and the establishment of it in the good opinion of the citizenship, that it may reflect their will)—these gentlemen are not non-partisan in motive or action, and we must devote ourselves as citizens to the continuous cause of good government for the three hundred and sixty-five days of each single year.

We are deeply grateful, we of the city of New York, to the Southern Society.   I have been intensely interested in the elaborate explanations that were made by some of the speakers as to why they were appropriately present to-night.   If it is not too late, I also have an explanation. My ancestors came from a country which also had a North and a South, and *mine* came from the South of Ireland.   And then I had an uncle, who did not get as far south as the Confederate army, but who, though born in the South of Ireland and reared in the City of New York, was put out of business three times for editing a Southern paper on Manhattan Island.

And so you see the Mayor of New York and some of his friends have not had to learn the art of offensive and defensive warfare.   It sort of runs in the veins, to speak out in town meeting, to have opinions, and to express them.

We owe the South much in the City of New York. We owe it for the temper that it has brought to our population, the good temper, the geniality, the manners, the warmth, the mellow disposition, and the beauty of the women of the South.

We have accomplished great things in the City of New York, because in the City of New York, you have not been Southerners except on occasions such as this. You have been New Yorkers for the honor of the City and the State. You have merged yourself into both the bone and sinew of a great cosmopolitan population. You have lived with the love of your traditional history, but with a knowledge of the duties of the present, and so you have helped to make New York the city that it is, the imperial municipality of the western hemisphere, and, gentlemen, New York is the most hospitable city in the world. She is receptive of the genius and the talent of the country, and she does not ask, "Come you from the East, from the South, or from the West, or from the North," but she says, "Have you got the talent and genius for coöperation? If you have, come in."

And so, you have all come in. Indeed, Major-General Barry, and John Mitchel and I, who happened by the accident of birth, over which we had no control, to be brought forth on Manhattan Island, are seriously contemplating the necessity of forming a society of "The Native Sons of Manhattan."

You know of no society for the perpetuation of the citizenship, the original citizenship, of New York. Why? Because it would be too provincial for the cosmopolitan spirit of New York. We love old Manhattan Island just as you love the South, and every State from which you have come. You have added to the prosperity; you have added to the civic virtue; you have added to the courage; you have added to the manhood of our city, and for these things we thank you, and when you think back into the distant past, if you think with me you see in the shining Eternal City the lined and gray-haired mothers of the Southland, those women who sacrificed all that their sons might battle for the things they felt were right, and you see those battle-scarred fathers, and sons, and husbands, and sweethearts in the gray mist of the Great Hereafter, in the sunlit cities of the Great Beyond, standing with smiles of benediction on their faces for the children of the new South, that you may do well here for the honor of a reunited country and for the accomplishment of an eternal destiny.

Gentlemen, the accomplishment of the things here are merely passing, as we know. The traditions of the past are the things that fire the blood for the purposes of peace. The men in serried ranks who fought the battles of our country fought in vain, if they did not fight to establish a permanent character of reunited, republican, peaceful form of government.

We know no South, we know no North. We shall know no East, and we shall know no West, but the men and the women of America, breathing the traditions of their ancestors, loving the institutions of their country, standing valiantly for continuous civic purity and governmental honesty, must coöperate for the perpetuation of the things for which the fathers and the mothers of the

North joined with the fathers and mothers of the South in the stirring episodes of history.

THE TOASTMASTER: I submit, gentlemen, that we have been enriched by the splendid addresses to which we have listened, and upon your behalf I extend to these gentlemen your profound gratitude.   I now declare this meeting adjourned.

HE New York Southern Society was formally organized in the City of New York on the 9th day of November, 1886, and incorporated under the laws of the State of New York in May, 1889.

CERTIFICATE OF INCORPORATION

STATE OF NEW YORK,
CITY OF NEW YORK, } ss.:
COUNTY OF NEW YORK,

We, John C. Calhoun, James H. Parker, William P. St. John, Evan Thomas, William L. Trenholm, Macgrane Coxe, Walter L. McCorkle, William G. Crenshaw, Jr., Charles A. Deshon, William W. Flannagan, George Rutledge Gibson, Robert L. Harrison, and James Swann, all of full age, citizens of the United States and of the State of New York, desiring to form ourselves and others into a Society for social, patriotic, historical, and literary purposes, pursuant to the provisions of an act entitled, "An Act for the incorporation of societies or clubs for certain lawful purposes," passed May 12, 1878, and the acts amendatory thereof and supplementary thereto, do hereby, for the purpose of incorporating such Society, certify as follows:

I. The name or title by which such Society shall be known in law is:

NEW YORK SOUTHERN SOCIETY.

II. The particular business or object of such Society shall be:

To cherish and perpetuate the memories and traditions of the Southern people and to cultivate friendly relations between the Southern men resident, or temporarily sojourning, in New York City.

III. The number of trustees, directors, or managers to manage the same shall be:

THIRTEEN

IV. The names of the trustees, directors, or managers for the first year of its existence shall be:

JOHN C. CALHOUN	WALTER L. MCCORKLE
JAMES H. PARKER	WILLIAM G. CRENSHAW, JR.
WILLIAM P. ST. JOHN	CHARLES A. DESHON
EVAN THOMAS	WILLIAM W. FLANNAGAN
WILLIAM L. TRENHOLM	GEORGE RUTLEDGE GIBSON
MACGRANE COXE	ROBERT L. HARRISON

JAMES SWANN

V. The principal office of said Society shall be located at the City of New York, in the County and State of New York.

Dated, New York, May 5, 1889,

NEW YORK SOUTHERN SOCIETY

JOHN C. CALHOUN
JAMES H. PARKER
WILLIAM P. ST. JOHN
EVAN THOMAS
WILLIAM L. TRENHOLM
MACGRANE COXE

WALTER L. MCCORKLE
WILLIAM G. CRENSHAW, JR.
CHARLES A. DESHON
WILLIAM W. FLANNAGAN
GEORGE RUTLEDGE GIBSON
ROBERT L. HARRISON
JAMES SWANN

CITY AND COUNTY OF NEW YORK, ⎱ SS.:
      STATE OF NEW YORK,   ⎰

On this 15th day of May, 1889, before me personally came John C. Calhoun, James H. Parker, William P. St. John, Evan Thomas, William L. Trenholm, Macgrane Coxe, Walter L. McCorkle, William G. Crenshaw, Jr., Charles A. Deshon, William W. Flannagan, George Rutledge Gibson, Robert L. Harrison, and James Swann, to me severally known and known to me to be the individuals described in and who executed the foregoing certificate and severally acknowledged to me that they executed the same.

James F. Doyle,
Notary Public, N. Y. Co.

(SEAL)

I, John R. Brady, one of the Justices of the Supreme Court for the Fifth District, do hereby approve of the within certificate and consent that the same be filed.
Dated, New York, May 16, 1889.

Jno. R. Brady.

57

Filed and recorded in the office of the Secretary of State, May 17, 1889.

Filed and recorded in the office of the Clerk of the City and County of New York, May 18, 1889.

CONSTITUTION

ARTICLE I

HE name of this Association is New York Southern Society.

ARTICLE II

The object of this Society is to promote friendly relations between Southern men resident or temporarily sojourning in New York City, and to cherish and perpetuate the memories and traditions of the Southern people.

ARTICLE III

SEC. 1. Any male over eighteen years of age, resident of, or having a permanent place of business in the City of New York, or within a radius of fifty miles, who was himself, or either of whose parents was born in the District of Columbia, or in any of the following States, namely: Delaware, Maryland, Virginia, West Virginia, North Carolina, South Carolina, Georgia, Florida, Alabama, Mississippi, Louisiana, Texas, Tennessee, Arkansas, Kentucky, or Missouri, and the male descendants of such persons, over eighteen years of age, to the third generation, shall be eligible to membership. (As amended May 9, 1903.)

SEC. 2. Any male over eighteen years of age, not a

resident of, nor having a permanent place of business in the City of New York, or within a radius of fifty miles, who was himself or either of whose parents was born in the District of Columbia, or in any of the following States, namely: Delaware, Maryland, Virginia, West Virginia, North Carolina, South Carolina, Georgia, Florida, Alabama, Mississippi, Louisiana, Texas, Tennessee, Arkansas, Kentucky, or Missouri, and the male descendants of such persons, over eighteen years of age, to the third generation, shall be eligible to non-resident membership and may be elected thereto in the same manner as resident members, and shall have all the privileges of resident members, save a vote at the meetings of the Society, and as herein otherwise restricted. (As amended May 9, 1903.)

SEC. 3. All applicants for membership shall be proposed by one member and seconded by another member of the Society, in writing.

SEC. 4. Membership shall be acquired upon approval and election by the Executive Committee and payment of the current dues. If an applicant for membership shall fail to pay the current dues within sixty days of the notice of his election by mail, addressed to him at the place given as his address in the application for membership, his election shall be void.

SEC. 5. In passing upon an application for membership, the Executive Committee shall vote by ballot, and two dissenting votes shall defeat the application.

SEC. 6. Resident members, on becoming non-residents, within the meaning of Section 2 of this article, may, on their option, become non-resident members— such option to be certified in writing to the Executive Committee; and non-resident members shall become resident members on establishing a residence within fifty miles of New York, and shall thereupon pay the proper dues of resident members. Ministers of the Gospel, without regard to residence, if otherwise qualified, may become non-resident members.

SEC. 7. That John Marshall be and is hereby made an honorary member of this Society in recognition of his services as originator and organizer of the same.

SEC. 8. Officers of the Army and Navy, now members, and those eligible to membership, who shall be hereafter elected, shall be considered as non-resident members, and when they are ordered on service outside the limits of the United States, or stationed to a post distant more than two hundred and fifty miles from New York, for a period longer than one year, their dues shall be remitted during the period of such service.

ARTICLE IV

OFFICERS

The officers of the Society shall be a President, a Vice-President, Secretary, and a Treasurer, who, with thirteen members until the Annual Meeting of 1896, and thereafter with twelve members, elected for the purpose, shall constitute the Executive Committee. The President, Vice-President, Secretary, and Treasurer shall be elected by ballot at the Annual Meeting in each year, to take office immediately upon election, and shall hold office for one year and until their successors are elected. Said thirteen members of the Executive Committee shall be elected at the Annual Meeting of 1895, by ballot, and shall immediately upon election divide themselves by lot into three classes, one class of five members to serve for one year and until their successors are elected, one class of four members to serve for two years and until their successors are elected, and one class of four members to serve for three years and until their successors are elected, and thereafter, beginning with the year 1896, four members of the Executive Committee shall be elected by ballot at each Annual Meeting to serve for a period of three years, until their successors are elected.

Non-resident members shall not be eligible to office or membership upon the Executive Committee.

ARTICLE V

PRESIDENT AND VICE-PRESIDENT

The President, and in his absence the Vice-President, shall preside at all meetings of the Society, and in the event of the absence of both President and Vice-President a meeting of the Society or of the Executive Committee may elect its presiding officer.

The President shall, with the Secretary, sign all written contracts and obligations of the Society, and shall perform such other duties as the Executive Committee and the Society shall assign them.

ARTICLE VI

TREASURER

The Treasurer shall collect all dues and claims of the Society, and shall deposit the same in a proper depository selected by the Executive Committee. He shall keep the accounts of the Society and report thereon at each regular meeting of the Executive Committee and of the Society.

His accounts. shall be audited by the Executive Committee semi-annually.

He shall pay all bills when certified as correct as prescribed by the Executive Committee. He shall notify persons elected to membership of their election. He shall sign all checks of the Society, unless otherwise provided by the Executive Committee.

ARTICLE VII

SECRETARY

The Secretary shall give notice of all meetings of the Society and of the Executive Committee, and shall keep the minutes of such meetings; he shall conduct the correspondence and keep the records of the Society.

He shall furnish to the Treasurer the names of all persons elected to membership, and shall be the keeper of the seal of the Society.

ARTICLE VIII

EXECUTIVE COMMITTEE

SEC. 1.   The Executive Committee shall adopt a proper seal for this Society, and shall have general charge of the affairs, funds, and property of the Society.

It shall have full power and it shall be its duty to carry out the purposes of the Society, according to its charter and constitution.   (As amended May 9, 1903.)

SEC. 2.   The Executive Committee shall have power to prescribe rules for the admission of strangers to the privileges of the Society.

SEC. 3.   The Executive Committee shall have power to fill all vacancies which shall occur in the offices of the Society for the unexpired term of such officer, and also to fill all vacancies in the membership of the Executive Committee until the next Annual Meeting, when an election will be held to fill any vacancies in the membership of the Executive Committee for the unexpired term of the member creating the vacancy.   The election of a member of the Executive Committee to office shall create a vacancy in the place of the member so elected.

SEC. 4. Any member of the Executive Committee who shall absent himself from three consecutive regular meetings, unless he shall have previously obtained permission so to do from the Committee, or shall present at the next regular meeting an excuse for his absence, satisfactory to each member of the Committee present, shall be deemed to have resigned.

SEC. 5. The Executive Committee may from time to time set apart moneys of the Society for the establishment and accumulation of a "Charity Fund," to which shall be added all donations and bequests thereto. Said fund shall be kept separately deposited in bank or invested in such manner as is permitted by law to trustees and savings banks, and it shall be used and paid out as directed by said committee for the assistance of the unfortunate and those in distress; provided, however, that during any fiscal year not more than the accumulated income and one fourth of any other additions during such year to said fund shall be disbursed. (As amended March 5, 1908.)

ARTICLE IX

MEETINGS

SEC. 1. There shall be an Annual Meeting of the Society on the first Thursday in March of each year, at such hour as the Executive Committee may designate.

Sec. 2. At all meetings of the Society, twenty-five regularly enrolled resident members of the Society shall constitute a quorum for the transaction of business.

If no quorum be present, the presiding officer shall adjourn the meeting to any other day, with the same effect as if held above.

Sec. 3. Special meetings of the Society may be called at any time by the Executive Committee, and upon the written request of twenty-five resident members the President, and in his absence the Vice-President, shall call a special meeting of the Society; the request for a special meeting, and also the notice of any special meeting, shall state the object for which the meeting is called, and at the special meeting any subject not so stated shall not be considered.

ARTICLE X

STANDING COMMITTEES

There shall be five standing Committees of the Society: Committee on Entertainment, Committee on Admissions, Committee on Speakers, and Auditing Committee; each of which shall consist of three members to be appointed annually by the President; and a Nominating Committee, consisting of five members, four of whom shall be elected by ballot at the Annual Meeting of each year, to hold office until the next Annual Meeting thereafter, and until their successors are elected. The fifth member of the Nominating Committee shall be a member of the Executive Committee and shall be appointed by that Committee as Chairman of the Nominating Committee. It shall be the duty of the Nominating Committee to nominate officers and members of the Executive Committee for the vacancies occurring at the next ensuing Annual Meeting after the election of the Nominating Committee. Vacancies in the Nominating Committee shall be filled by that Committee. It shall be the duty of the Secretary to print and mail with the notice of each Annual Meeting, at least twenty days before the meeting, a ticket containing the nominations proposed by the Nominating Committee.

This method of nomination shall not be deemed to exclude any other nominations, when made by at least five members of the Society, upon ten days' notice thereof being sent by the Secretary to the resident members of the Society, nor the right to nominate *viva voce* at the Annual Meeting.

Additional committees may be appointed in the discretion of the Executive Committee. The Executive Committee shall have power to remove at any time any member of committees appointed by it. (As amended April 7, 1905.)

ARTICLE XI

AUDITING COMMITTEE

The Auditing Committee shall audit the accounts of the Treasurer semi-annually, and report to the Executive Committee the accounts audited and allowed since their previous report.

They may also act as a Finance Committee, with such duties and powers as the Executive Committee may prescribe.

ARTICLE XII

COMMITTEE ON ADMISSIONS

The Committee on Admissions shall examine into and report to the Executive Committee upon the qualifications of any candidate for admission into the Society.

ARTICLE XIII

The Society shall, as soon as may be practicable, establish a Library, which shall be confined, as far as possible, to those works which relate to the history and literature of the South, in order that it may portray the character and genius, and perpetuate the memories and traditions of the Southern people.

ARTICLE XIV

INITIATION FEES AND DUES

SEC. 1. The annual dues for resident members shall be ten dollars, and for non-resident members, five dollars, payable annually in advance on the first day of November in each year. But members elected within one month of the end of the current fiscal year shall, in all cases, be exempt from payment of dues for the unexpired portion of the fiscal year in which they are elected.

SEC. 2. When the dues of any member shall remain unpaid for the space of two months, the Treasurer shall cause him to be notified by mail, and if he fails to pay within one month thereafter, he shall cease to be a member, without any action of the Executive Committee; but he may be reinstated by a vote of a majority of the members of the Executive Committee present at any regular meeting.

SEC. 3. Any member who shall fail to pay any amount due by him to the Society, except dues, for one month after the notice of the indebtedness, requesting payment of the same, may be dropped from the membership by a majority vote of the members of the Executive Committee present at any regular meeting, but he may be reinstated by a like vote.

SEC. 4. Upon payment of the sum of $200, any member shall be entitled to a certificate, signed by the

President and countersigned by the Treasurer of the Society, to the effect that such a member is a life member of the Society, and exempt from further dues, provided, however, that such certificates outstanding at any one time shall not exceed one hundred in number.

Any member who has rendered distinguished and unusual service to the Society may be elected a life member by the unanimous vote of the Executive Committee. (As amended March 3, 1910.)

ARTICLE XV

CENSURE, SUSPENSION, AND EXPULSION

Any member may be censured, suspended, or expelled for a violation of the constitution or a rule, or for any conduct not in violation of tʰe constitution or a rule which in the opinion of the Executive Committee is improper and prejudicial to the welfare or reputation of the Society, by a vote of three fourths of the members of the Executive Committee present at a meeting, ten days' previous notice, in writing, having been given to the member, with a copy of the charge against him.

ARTICLE XVI

RESIGNATIONS

Resignations of membership shall be made to the Secretary in writing, which shall be accepted, provided all indebtedness to the Society shall have been paid by such member, and such member shall be in good standing at the time of offering his resignation.

ARTICLE XVII

AMENDMENTS

The Constitution may be amended at any annual meeting of the Society, or special meeting called for the purpose, by a two-thirds vote in the affirmative, a quorum being present and voting.

Notice of proposed amendments shall be furnished to the Secretary at least fifteen days before the meeting at which it is proposed to consider them, and the Secretary shall cause such notice to be printed and sent to each member at least ten days before such meeting.

BY-LAWS

SEC. 1. At the regular meetings of the Society, the order of business shall be as follows:

1. Reading of minutes.
2. Unfinished business.
3. Report of Executive Committee.
4. Report of Treasurer.
5. Reports of Special Committees.
6. Miscellaneous business.

SEC. 2. At regular meetings of the Executive Committee the order of business shall be:

1. Roll call.
2. Reading of minutes.
3. Unfinished business.
4. Report of Treasurer.
5. Report of Auditing Committee.
6. Report of Committee on Admissions.
7. Election of members.
8. Report of House Committee.
9. `Report of Committee on Literature and Art.
10. Reports of Special Committees.
11. Miscellaneous business.

ACCOUNTS AND BOOKS

SEC. 3.   The Treasurer shall report in writing to the Executive Committee at their first meeting in each month a balance sheet, and every existing appropriation which may effect the same.   He shall also report at such meetings the number of members in good standing and the names of those in arrears.

At the Annual Meeting of the Society he shall make a full report of the receipts and disbursements of the past fiscal year, suitably classified, and of all outstanding obligations of the Society.   He shall keep regular accounts in books belonging to the Society.   The books of the Secretary and Treasurer shall be kept in the rooms of the Society.

SEC. 4.   No member of the Executive Committee shall propose or second an applicant.   All applicants for Resident Membership must be personally known to at least two members of the Executive Committee.   The proposer and seconder of a Non-Resident Member must be personally known to at least two members of the Committee.

HUGH R. GARDEN LIBRARY

Through a donation from the late Mr. Hugh R. Garden, the Society is possessed of a library which is the best collection of Southern literature in the City of New York. This library has been deposited in the Library of Columbia University, where the members of the Society have access not only to the books of the Society library but also to those of the Library of Columbia University.

LIFE MEMBERS

Name	State of Birth or Descent
Abney, John R.	South Carolina
Adams, Henry C.	Virginia
Agar, John G.	Louisiana
Beall, Turner A.	Maryland
Bertron, S. R.	Mississippi
Calhoun, Patrick.	South Carolina
Carpenter, Nathaniel Leslie.	Mississippi
Clarke, R. Floyd	South Carolina
Coxe, Macgrane.	Alabama
Deshon, Charles A.	Alabama
Einstein, B. F.	Texas
Flannagan, W. W.	Virginia
French, Dr. John H.	Virginia
Gatins, Joseph F.	Georgia
Haines, H. S.	South Carolina
Hardy, Gaston.	Virginia
Harrison, Robert L.	Virginia
Hobbs, Elon S.	Maryland
Jones, W. Strother	Virginia
King, John.	Virginia
McAdoo, Hon. William G.	Georgia
McChesney, John T.	Virginia
McCorkle, Walter L.	Virginia
Marshall, John (Honorary)	Virginia
Maury, C. W.	Virginia
Myles, Dr. Robert C.	Mississippi

Nash, E. S...North Carolina

Osborne, James W..................................North Carolina

Page, Thomas Nelson................................Virginia
Parker, Dr. James H...............................North Carolina
Peabody, George Foster.............................Georgia
Pickrell, Percy A.................................Virginia
Polk, Dr. William M...............................Tennessee
Price, Theodore H.................................Virginia

Read, Dr. Henry N.................................Virginia
Roddey, John T....................................South Carolina
Ryan, Thomas F....................................Virginia

Salomon, William..................................South Carolina
Sharp, W. W.......................................Virginia
Springs, Richard A................................South Carolina
Stebbins, Charles J...............................Louisiana
Sullivan, George H................................Virginia

Tilford, Henry M..................................Kentucky

Verdery, Marion J.................................Georgia

Watkins, B. F.....................................North Carolina
Worman, Dr. J. H..................................South Carolina
Wyeth, Dr. John A.................................Alabama
Wylie, Dr. W. Gill................................South Carolina

RESIDENT MEMBERS

Name	State of Birth or Descent
Abraham, Dr. Joseph H.	Alabama
Adair, W. T.	Missouri
Adamson, Robert	Georgia
Aiken, D. Wyatt	Georgia
Alexander, Chester	Alabama
Alexander, William	Virginia
Allen, Charles Seldon	Virginia
Allen, James A.	Kentucky
Allen, J. F.	Georgia
Allen, William	Virginia
Allen, Dr. W. B.	South Carolina
Alley, Rayford Wardlow	Tennessee
Altsheler, Joseph Alexander	Kentucky
Anderson, Dr. Augustus Milton	Georgia
Anderson, Edgar T.	Tennessee
Anderson, John I.	Kentucky
Andrews, Charles Lee	Maryland
Anthony, Thomas Gill	Virginia
Armstrong, David Wilson, Jr.	Kentucky
Artaud, Theodore P.	Mississippi
Atkins, George W. E.	Tennessee
Atkinson, George C.	Georgia
Austell, Erle Lochrane	Georgia
Ayer, Dr. J. M.	North Carolina
Baggett, Shelley I.	Georgia
Baker, DeWitt C.	Texas
Baker, Edward Y.	Virginia
Baker, Keith Lanneau	Mississippi
Baker, Thomas K.	Virginia
Baldwin, Frank V.	Virginia
Baldwin, W. H.	Maryland
Ball, Alwyn, Jr.	South Carolina
Ball, Eustace Hale	Virginia
Ball, James W.	Virginia
Barber, William A.	South Carolina

77

Barnett, Bion Hall, Jr......................................Florida
Barney, J. Stewart.......................................Virginia
Barnum, Charles K..Georgia
Barrows, Dr. Charles C...................................Mississippi
Barrows, Dr. David Nye...................................Mississippi
Bartels, J. Murray.......................................Virginia
Baruch, Dr. Simon..South Carolina
Baskerville, Dr. Charles.................................Mississippi
Bass, Walter A...Virginia
Batchelor, O. D..North Carolina
Bateman, Jas. Goldsborough...............................Maryland
Bates, Wm. C...Tennessee
Bateson, C. E. W...Louisiana
Bateson, Richard H.......................................Louisiana
Battle, George Gordon....................................North Carolina
Bayne, Daniel K..Virginia
Bayne, Hon. Howard R.....................................Virginia
Bayne, Lawrence Pope.....................................Virginia
Bayne, Walter L..Maryland
Beach, George F..Virginia
Beale, Phelan..Alabama
Beall, Jeremiah..Georgia
Beaty, Julian B..South Carolina
Beckman, Alfred H..Kentucky
Becton, M. W...North Carolina
Bell, Dr. George Huston..................................Virginia
Bell, Oliver L...Maryland
Bibb, William G..Alabama
Bigelow, Edwin H...District of Columbia
Billups, John M., Jr.....................................Mississippi
Bishop, John G...Virginia
Black, William Harman....................................Georgia
Blair, Walter Dabney.....................................Virginia
Blow, A. A...Virginia
Bodine, Dr. John A.......................................Kentucky
Borden, Herbert L..North Carolina
Boston, Charles A..Maryland
Bower, J. D..Georgia
Bowman, Walker...Virginia
Boyer, Norman..Maryland
Bozeman, Dr. Nathan G....................................Alabama
Brady, Charles D...Georgia

78

Bragg, H. Lee...Virginia
Branch, James R..Virginia
Brander, John A..Virginia
Brander, T. W...Virginia
Brannon, R. M...Georgia
Brauer, William W.......................................Virginia
Breckenridge, Geo. P.....................................Missouri
Breckinridge, John C.....................................Kentucky
Breckinridge, Lucian S..................................Kentucky
Breed, George Horace....................................Kentucky
Breitenbach, Max J......................................Georgia
Brennecke, Sidney B..............................South Carolina
Brent, Henry K..Kentucky
Britton, Mason...Virginia
Brooks, Belvidere..Texas
Brooks, Belvidere, Jr......................................Texas
Broughton, Wm. H. C...................................Mississippi
Broun, Dr. LeRoy..Virginia
Brown, Dr. Richard Ewell...............................Tennessee
Brown, Robert Rankins...................................Alabama
Bryan, Charles S..................................North Carolina
Bryan, Reginald M.......................................Georgia
Buck, Gordon M.......................................Mississippi
Buckner, Mortimer N....................................Louisiana
Buckner, Thomas A......................................Kentucky
Buckner, William D......................................Virginia
Buhler, Joseph S..Georgia
Burckel, John A...Georgia
Burroughs, A. H...Virginia
Burton, S. W..Virginia

Cabell, P. Mason,..Virginia
Caffey, Francis G..Alabama
Caldwell, Dr. Eugene W..................................Missouri
Caldwell, Hugh H.................................North Carolina
Caldwell, James Hope....................................Georgia
Calhoun, John C..................................South Carolina
Campbell, Edwin, Jr.....................................Virginia
Campbell, W. R..Kentucky
Campe, Emanuel N.......................................Virginia
Carhart, J. D...Virginia
Carr, A. Marvin..................................North Carolina

Carr, Dr. Matthew L. . . . . North Carolina
Carr, Thomas Wood. . . . . Virginia
Carroll, Edward, Jr. . . . . South Carolina
Carroll, Ephraim Mikell. . . . . South Carolina
Carroll, J. Pratt. . . . . Maryland
Carstarphen, Frank E. . . . . Missouri
Carter, Dr. William Wesley. . . . . North Carolina
Cash, Dr. S. Langford. . . . . South Carolina
Cassard, Jules. . . . . Louisiana
Cassell, Dr. James Wilson. . . . . Kentucky
Catchings, Benjamin S. . . . . Tennessee
Cayce, A. B. . . . . Virginia
Chambers, Frank R. . . . . Alabama
Chambers, Dr. P. F. . . . . Alabama
Chapman, C. Brewster. . . . . Georgia
Chapman, Charles McC. . . . . District of Columbia
Cherry, William I. . . . . Tennessee
Chisholm, Edward de C. . . . . Georgia
Claiborne, Dr. J. Herbert. . . . . Virginia
Clark, Burnet L. . . . . Alabama
Clark, Edward H. . . . . Missouri
Claybrook, Richard A. . . . . Virginia
Clayton, Joseph Culbertson. . . . . Virginia
Clayton, R. R. . . . . Virginia
Clendenin, Joseph. . . . . Maryland
Cleveland, George W. . . . . Texas
Cobb, Irvin Shrewsbury. . . . . Kentucky
Cobb, John B. . . . . North Carolina
Cochran, John L. . . . . Tennessee
Cocke, Nathaniel C. . . . . Virginia
Cocke, Dr. William Irby. . . . . Texas
Coffin, Charles H. . . . . Tennessee
Cohen, J. Quintus. . . . . South Carolina
Cohen, Louis M. . . . . Georgia
Colby, Bainbridge. . . . . Missouri
Coleman, Richard Marshall. . . . . Virginia
Coleman, Dr. Warren. . . . . Georgia
Collens, J. C. W. . . . . Louisiana
Collier, Barron G. . . . . Tennessee
Collins, Loyd A. . . . . Georgia
Collins, William R. . . . . Georgia
Colville, Fulton. . . . . Tennessee

Colvin, Grattan..Georgia
Compton, William Norris..............................Alabama
Conger, Stephen D......................................Texas
Conley, William W....................................Missouri
Connelly, Edmond J...................................Alabama
Cook, Howard B..Georgia
Cooper, James S......................................Louisiana
Cooper, Sam. Bronson..............................Kentucky
Cootes, F. Graham.....................................Virginia
Corbin, Floyd S..Georgia
Cothran, C. H..Georgia
Covington, George B..................................Maryland
Cowan, Charles C....................................Mississippi
Cowles, Dr. Henry C............................North Carolina
Cox, John W..Mississippi
Cox, Raymond B......................................Maryland
Craft, James Charles..........................North Carolina
Craig, Robert E., Jr................................Mississippi
Craig, William R....................................Mississippi
Craighill, Edward A., Jr..............................Virginia
Crank, J. M..Texas
Crawford, Robert L..................................Alabama
Craycroft, Robert Lee...............................Maryland
Crichton, Powell....................................Louisiana
Crigler, Dr. Lewis Webb.............................Mississippi
Crook, J. D..Texas
Cross, George D.......................................Florida
Crump, Dr. Armistead C...............................Virginia
Cudlipp, Frederick Olof..............................Virginia
Cumming, James D...............................North Carolina
Cumming, Preston, Jr..........................North Carolina
Cunningham, S. A....................................Kentucky

Dale, James Lowry....................................Alabama
Daly, Hon. Joseph F...........................North Carolina
Daniel, John G.................................North Carolina
Daniel, Phocion M...................................Kentucky
Davis, Dr. Achilles Edward.........................Kentucky
Davis, Dr. E. Webster................................Alabama
Davis, Dr. George E.................................Kentucky
Davis, J. Winter....................................Maryland
Davis, Maurice E....................................Kentucky

Davis, William Benson..............................Maryland
Dawson, Edgar......................................Virginia
Dayhoff, Samuel R.................................Maryland
Dean, James Wallace...............................Tennessee
Dear, Dr. S. Brock McG.............................Virginia
Deems, Dr. J. Harry, Jr............................Maryland
DeKnight, Edward W...................District of Columbia
DeLeon, Edwin W.............................South Carolina
Dent, T. Ashley...................................Maryland
Dent, William E.................................Mississippi
Dickinson, Fairleigh S.......................North Carolina
Dinwiddie, James H.................................Virginia
Ditto, W. A. B....................................Maryland
Dixon, Walter E.....................................Georgia
Dobbins, J. P.....................................Tennessee
Dold, Dr. William Elliott..........................Virginia
Doniphan, John V................................Mississippi
Dorsey, J. Worthington............................Maryland
Dorsey, Richard M.................................Maryland
Dortch, B. W......................................Tennessee
Drake, Benjamin S...................................Georgia
Duckworth, Lenn A..................................Kentucky
Dudley, Ralph......................................Georgia
Duncan, Oscar Dibble...............................Alabama
Dunham, L. A.......................................Kentucky
Dunlop, James N....................................Virginia
Dunn, Beverly Wyly................................Louisiana
Dunn, Charles J....................................Georgia
Dunn, Frederick C..................................Virginia
Dunn, Robert Lee..................................Tennessee

Early, Ernest Rhea.................................Virginia
East, John P.......................................Virginia
Eastman, Frank Carr...............................Tennessee
Edgar, Maurice L...................................Maryland
Edgerton, Dr. J. Ives........................South Carolina
Edwards, Evan S.................................Mississippi
Edwards, James M...................................Georgia
Edwards, Tryon Pierrepont.........................Maryland
Eldridge, Herbert R..................................Texas
Elliott, Robert W. B...............................Georgia
Emerson, Dr. Charles H...........................Louisiana

82

Emerson, Isaac E.................................North Carolina
Emory, J. C..Maryland
Enslow, Joseph Aquilla.........................South Carolina
Eskridge, Jefferson L...........................North Carolina
Essig, Erskine Birch..................................Missouri
Evans, David Lewis, 5th............................Tennessee
Evans, Henry..Texas
Evans, Walter E.......................................Georgia
Everett, Joseph H.................................North Carolina

Fagan, William R...................................Louisiana
Fain, Wm. H..Tennessee
Faison, John W...................................North Carolina
Faulkner, Daniel R..................................Maryland
Fearons, George H..................................Kentucky
Ferguson, Wynne...................................Tennessee
Fickling, W. Irvine......................District of Columbia
Field, Albert C.....................................Kentucky
Field, Francis L.....................................Virginia
Fiery, Edgar I......................................Maryland
Filley, F. Herbert...................................Missouri
Finch, Fenton F.....................................Virginia
Finerty, Wm. J......................................Alabama
Fish, Stuyvesant................................South Carolina
Fitch, Dr. William Edward.....................North Carolina
Fitzhugh, Dr. Patrick Henry........................Virginia
Fitzwilson, W. G....................................Virginia
Flaherty, Thomas P.................................Louisiana
Fleming, Lamar L....................................Georgia
Fletcher, James, Jr.................................Maryland
Flinn, Robert Browder..............................Kentucky
Flowers, Arthur H...................................Alabama
Ford, David..Georgia
Ford, Lawrence D...................................Maryland
Foulk, Thomas Bond ....Maryland
Fowler, Frederick.................................Mississippi
Frank, Ashbrook C..................................Kentucky
Frank, H. Seaton...................................Maryland
Frank, Henry Seymour...............................Maryland
Frazer, Jos. Washington...........................Tennessee
Frazier, Frederic H............................West Virginia
Freeman, Edward D.................................Tennessee

Freeman, John Strother..............................Virginia
Freeman, Roy Bolton.........................South Carolina
Fry, Charles Philip....................................Alabama
Fuller, Bayard C...............................South Carolina
Fuller, Clifford J....................................Tennessee
Fuller, Thomas Staples......................North Carolina
Fuller, W. W...................................North Carolina
Fultz, David L...Virginia
Furniss, Dr. Henry Dawson...........................Alabama

Gadd, Luther Lay....................................Maryland
Gaillard, Frank P.............................South Carolina
Gaillard, M. H..Kentucky
Gaillard, William D...........................South Carolina
Gaillard, William E. G..............................Kentucky
Gaines, Henry Venable................................Virginia
Gaines, Dr. John Strother, Jr......................Kentucky
Gaines, Richard Heyward..............................Virginia
Gaines, T. Foster.-..................................Virginia
Gaither, Harry W....................................Maryland
Gale, Thomas B..Alabama
Gales, George M...............................North Carolina
Gallaher, Maurice....................................Virginia
Gant, Dr. Samuel G...................................Missouri
Gardner, Frank B.....................................Alabama
Garrison, Henry J...................................Kentucky
Gary, Chas. Braxton...........................North Carolina
Gary, W. Eugene, Jr..................................Virginia
Gatling, Norborne P...........................North Carolina
Gibb, William T......................................Virginia
Gibboney, Stuart G...................................Virginia
Gibney, Dr. Virgil P................................Kentucky
Gibson, Robert, Jr...................................Georgia
Gillette, John Kindred...............................Virginia
Gilmore, Dr. Samuel P...............................Kentucky
Glenn, John M.......................................Maryland
Glenn, William A..............................North Carolina
Glover, Frank D.....................................Kentucky
Gold, Pleasant D., Jr.........................North Carolina
Goodin, Philip T...................................Louisiana
Goodloe, J. S. M....................................Kentucky
Gordon, Richard Haden, Jr..........................Tennessee

Goss, H. L. . . . . South Carolina
Gossett, Thomas Henry. . . . . South Carolina
Gott, O. Wilson. . . . . Maryland
Grace, Dr. Thomas M. . . . . Georgia
Graham, T. Bertrand. . . . . Kentucky
Graham, William J. . . . . Kentucky
Granberry, George D. . . . . Mississippi
Granbery, Joseph A. . . . . Maryland
Graves, John Temple. . . . . South Carolina
Gray, Charles Stockdell. . . . . Georgia
Graybill, James Edward. . . . . Georgia
Green, Thos. D. . . . . South Carolina
Green, Wharton. . . . . Mississippi
Gregg, Charles W. . . . . Texas
Gresham, Wm. B. . . . . Georgia
Gress, John Hart. . . . . Georgia
Grimball, DeLancy I. . . . . South Carolina
Groscup, Frederick Nelson. . . . . Maryland
Gross, Albert H. . . . . Mississippi
Grubbs, Hartwell B. . . . . Alabama
Grubbs, Thomas C. . . . . Tennessee
Grymes, Arthur J. . . . . Virginia
Gudger, Francis A. . . . . North Carolina
Guggenheimer, Charles S. . . . . Virginia
Gwathmey, Archibald B. . . . . Virginia
Gwathmey, C. Browne. . . . . Virginia
Gwathmey, Dr. James T. . . . . Virginia
Gwathmey, J. Temple. . . . . Virginia
Gwathmey, R. W. . . . . Virginia
Gwyn, James A. . . . . North Carolina
Gwynn, Joseph K. . . . . Kentucky

Hager, Robert, Jr. . . . . Maryland
Haggin, James B. . . . . Kentucky
Hall, Frank G. . . . . Missouri
Hall, J. W. . . . . Virginia
Hallett, Allen P. . . . . North Carolina
Hamilton, Charles R. . . . . Tennessee
Hammond, Claude Randall. . . . . Georgia
Hammond, Hon. John Hays. . . . . Maryland
Hampton, Ellis H. . . . . Virginia
Hancock, Austin F. . . . . North Carolina

85

Hancock, Dr. Charles R.............................Virginia
Hand, G. C......................................North Carolina
Hanline, William M.................................Maryland
Hanway, Walter L...................................Maryland
Hardin, A. T...................................South Carolina
Hardin, Charles W.................................Tennessee
Hardin, Thomas B...................................Kentucky
Harding, George C.....................................Texas
Hardy, Willoughby D..........................North Carolina
Hargett, Dr. Arthur V..............................Maryland
Harman, Edward V...................................Virginia
Harman, John F...............................West Virginia
Harnsberger, Robert S..............................Virginia
Harper, Donald......................................Georgia
Harper, John H.....................................Virginia
Harrington, Frank T.................................Georgia
Harrington, John M..................................Georgia
Harris, Isaac F.............................North Carolina
Harrison, Henry Francis............................Maryland
Harrison, Thomas B., Jr............................Kentucky
Harriss, H. H..............................North Carolina
Harriss, William Leslie................................Texas
Hart, James Hamilton........................South Carolina
Hartfield, Joseph M...............................Kentucky
Hartmann, George N.................................Georgia
Hartridge, Julian...................................Georgia
Harty, Egbert R............................North Carolina
Harty, Frank R.............................North Carolina
Harwood, Franklin A................................Virginia
Hatch, Robert Lee...............................Mississippi
Hatcher, Halley...................................Virginia
Hatton, Clarence R................................Virginia
Havey, Marshall L.................................Tennessee
Hay, Edwin Barrett, Jr............................Maryland
Haythe, R. O......................................Virginia
Haywood, Alfred W., Jr......................North Carolina
Haywood, T. Holt...........................North Carolina
Hazzard, Elliott W.........................South Carolina
Hendrick, John Harris..............................Kentucky
Hendrick, William Jackson..........................Kentucky
Henry, Robert Braxton..............................Virginia
Henry, Ryder.......................................Maryland

Herbert, Preston...Georgia
Hernsheim, Isidore.....................................Mississippi
Hernsheim, Joseph......................................Louisiana
Hester, Charles R.......................................Kentucky
Hicks, J. M. W....................................North Carolina
Hicks, Thomas E..................................North Carolina
Hicks, Walter Clifton....................................Alabama
Higgins, Richard H.....................................Kentucky
Hill, Charles Willard..................................Tennessee
Hill, J. C..Arkansas
Hill, Leonard L...Virginia
Hill, Thos......................................North Carolina
Hines, Walker D..Kentucky
Hinkley, Bainbridge....................................Maryland
Hobbs, F. Hamilton.....................................Maryland
Hobbs, Col. John F...............................South Carolina
Hodson, Clarence.......................................Maryland
Hoffman, Charles R.....................................Kentucky
Holbrook, Henry F......................................Maryland
Holloway, William E.....................................Alabama
Homer, Francis T.......................................Maryland
Houston, Alfred..Delaware
Howe, George..Louisiana
Howell, Logan D.................................North Carolina
Howze, Wm. Heath................................South Carolina
Hoyle, Frank Jerome.....................................Georgia
Hoyt, William Henry.............................North Carolina
Humphreys, Dr. Gustavus A...............................Arkansas
Hunt, J. Hamilton...............................South Carolina
Hutchins, James M....................................Tennessee
Hutchinson, Cary T.....................................Missouri
Hutchinson, William F...................................Florida
Huvelle, Dr. Rene H......................................Texas
Hyde, Henry St. John....................................Alabama

Ijams, John Tabb.......................................Virginia
Ingle, Julian E., Jr...................................Maryland
Ivey, J. R. Graves......................................Alabama

Jackson, George P......................................Virginia
James, Charles Cooper.................................Tennessee
James, Dr. Robert Coleman..............................Kentucky

Jamison, Bernard A.............................Maryland
Jamison, J. Gough.............................Maryland
Janes, Charles K..............................Georgia
Janes, R. Ralph...............................Georgia
Jernigan, Dr. George F........................Tennessee
Johnson, Albert Livingston....................Maryland
Johnson, J. P.................................Virginia
Johnson, James S..........................West Virginia
Johnson, Joseph, Jr...........................Georgia
Jones, Arthur H............................Mississippi
Jones, George O........................North Carolina
Jones, Joseph S...............................Virginia
Jones, Leonard R..............................Maryland
Jones, Paul...................................Arkansas
Jones, Paul, Jr................................Texas
Jones, Richard Walter, Jr.....................Virginia
Jones, William A..............................Alabama
Jordon, Dr. Stroud.....................North Carolina
Judd, B. A......................................Texas
Judkins, William Duncan.......................Virginia

Kauffman, George A..............................Texas
Keebler, Roy Carter...........................Kentucky
Keeling, George W.............................Georgia
Keep, Henry V..............................Mississippi
Kelly, Samuel E...............................Kentucky
Kemp, Charles B...............................Kentucky
Kerrison, Dr. Philip D...................South Carolina
Key, Dr. Ben Witt.............................Georgia
Kight, Alonzo B........................North Carolina
Kindred, Dr. J. Joseph........................Virginia
King, John Allen.............................Tennessee
Kinney, Beirne................................Virginia
Kirtland, Michel..............................Alabama
Klein, William M.............................Louisiana
Klipstein, William A..........................Virginia
Kuhnast, Frederick E....................South Carolina

Lake, Harper...............................Mississippi
Lamb, Thomas Avery..........................Tennessee
Lamkin, Harry Tobin...........................Alabama
LaMonte, George M.............................Virginia

LaMotte, L. Howell.....................................Maryland
Lancaster, Edwin R.....................................Virginia
Lancaster, E. W..Virginia
Lane, Alfred Page......................................Virginia
Langford, Wm. H..Arkansas
Langhorne, Edmund G....................:...............Virginia
Latimer, M. G.....................................North Carolina
Lauderdale, T. W...................................South Carolina
Lavender, John G......................................Tennessee
Lawrence, Charles E................................South Carolina
Lawrence, Frank M..................................North Carolina
Lawson, Ben..North Carolina
Lawton, William M..................................South Carolina
Ledoux, Augustus D....................................Louisiana
Lee, Dr. George Bolling...............................Virginia
Lee, Richard Bland....................................Virginia
Leigh, Word...Georgia
Leland, Hume..Alabama
Leslie, John C....................................North Carolina
Levy, Charles E....................................Mississippi
Levy, Jefferson M.....................................Virginia
Lewis, George W.................................West Virginia
Lewis, R. E. Lee......................................Virginia
Lewis, Robert Proud...................................Maryland
Lifsey, W. V..Georgia
Ligon, William Daniel.................................Virginia
Lindsay, Dr. Harley B..............................South Carolina
Littleton, Hon. Martin W..............................Tennessee
Locher, Charles H.....................................Virginia
Logan, Alexander S....................................Georgia
Logan, Gen. T. M......................................Virginia
Long, Eugene McLean...................................Virginia
Lonsdale, John G......................................Tennessee
Lorton, Heth..Virginia
Love, John H..Kentucky
Lovett, Hon. Robert Scott...............................Texas
Lowe, John Z., Jr.....................................Virginia
Luckett, Dr. W. H.......................................Texas
Luellen, Lawrence W.............................West Virginia
Luke, David L...Delaware
Luke, Edwin C...Virginia
Lumb, Henry A......................................South Carolina

Lusk, Dr. Thurston Gilman...........................Alabama
Lynn, John..Alabama
Lyons, Howard J....................................Louisiana

McAfee, Claude M...................................Georgia
McAllister, A. S...................................Virginia
McAnerney, John....................................Alabama
McBee, Silas...................................North Carolina
McCalla, C. Wayne, Jr..............................Georgia
McCartney, Frank L.................................Virginia
McCarty, William F. M..............................Virginia
McCombs, William F., Jr............................Arkansas
McCorkle, Henry H..................................Virginia
McCoy, Paul....................................West Virginia
McDowell, E. Irvine................................Kentucky
McElroy, Hugh F...................................Louisiana
McMillin, Emerson..................................Virginia
McNeal, Austin....................................Tennessee
McReynolds, Hon. James C...........................Kentucky
McRoberts, Samuel..................................Missouri
Maas, Charles O...................................Louisiana
MacFadyean, James G..............................Mississippi
Machen, Thomas G..................................Maryland
Mack, William..................................South Carolina
Mackey, D. Clinton................................Maryland
MacRae, Dr. Thomas....................................Texas
Macrery, Andrew...................................Tennessee
Magnus, Percy C....................................Georgia
Malevinsky, Moses L..................................Texas
Mallett, Dr. George H.........................North Carolina
Mallett, Percy S..................................Louisiana
Marchant, Russell B...............................Virginia
Marchbanks, Hal......................................Texas
Marriott, James C.................................Maryland
Marriott, John H..................................Kentucky
Marshall, Charles Clay............................Virginia
Marshall, Finis E.................................Missouri
Marshall, Hon. H. Snowden.........................Maryland
Marshall, J. Markham..............................Maryland
Marshall, Walton H................................Virginia
Martin, Clarence D.................................Georgia
Martin, W. D..................................North Carolina

Mason, Lambert...Virginia
Massey, Albert..Maryland
Matchett, Charles C.....................................Delaware
Mayo, Hon. John B......................................Virginia
Meacham, George W...............................North Carolina
Meacham, Malcolm L................................Mississippi
Meader, Herman Lee....................................Louisiana
Meadows, Thomas E......................................Alabama
Meany, Edward P.......................................Kentucky
Mebane, Frank C...................................North Carolina
Meng, James S..Louisiana
Middleton, John A......................................Maryland
Miller, Edward C.......................................Alabama
Miller, Hugh Gordon....................................Virginia
Miller, John H...Virginia
Miller, Percival W................................South Carolina
Milnor, Bennett..Maryland
Milnor, M. Cleiland...............................South Carolina
Milnor, William H......................................Maryland
Minis, Robert Beverley..................................Georgia
Mitchell, Sidney Z......................................Alabama
Monroe, Robert Grier..................................Kentucky
Montgomery, Chas. S..Texas
Moody, Dr. L. Mason...................................Tennessee
Moore, Carey A..Maryland
Moore, Charles Forest.............................West Virginia
Moore, Harlan...Kentucky
Moore, Hugh E...Virginia
Moore, John N..Virginia
Morgan, Coleman......................................Kentucky
Morgan, Robert M.......................................Virginia
Morrison, Dr. Eugene T....................................Texas
Morrow, Dr. Albert S..................................Kentucky
Mountjoy, Wilbert W....................................Virginia
Munds, James Theus...............................North Carolina
Munford, Irving H....................................Tennessee
Murphy, Dr. Deas.......................................Alabama
Murphy, Dr. W. A.......................................Virginia
Myers, John Caldwell...................................Alabama
Myers, Joseph G..Virginia
Myers, Joseph G., Jr...................................Virginia
Myrick, Julian S..................................North Carolina

Naret, Charles C..................................Virginia
Neale, G. Brent..................................Maryland
Neel, William H............................North Carolina
Neilson, Thomas Hall..............................Virginia
Nelms, Bernard..................................Virginia
Nelson, Francis Kinloch..........................Maryland
Nelson, George E.................................Virginia
Nelson, J. C....................................Alabama
Newell, James Scarborough.........................Virginia
Nicolson, John..................................Georgia
Nisbet, Dr. J. Douglas......................South Carolina
Nixon, Lewis....................................Virginia
Noble, Herbert..................................Maryland
Norton, Ex......................................Kentucky

O'Connor, Gerald H..............................Louisiana
Ochs, Adolph S..................................Tennessee
Oeland, Isaac R.............................South Carolina
Oglesby, Albert S................................Kentucky
Orgain, Roy..Texas
Orne, Henry Merrill.............................Tennessee

Page, Dr. John Randolph..........................Virginia
Page, Hon. Walter H........................North Carolina
Palmer, J. Stacy.................................Virginia
Parker, Bedell..................................Georgia
Parker, John Scott..............................Alabama
Parker, Junius.............................North Carolina
Parrott, Marcus J..............................Tennessee
Parsons, Erastus J..............................Alabama
Paschall, Edward E.........................North Carolina
Pasco, Samuel Nash................................Florida
Patterson, George Elliott.........................Florida
Patterson, Rufus L.........................North Carolina
Paxton, Edward Gibbs..........................Mississippi
Paxton, Henry C..............................Mississippi
Payne, Dr. Sanders McA..........................Tennessee
Paynter, Richard K...............................Virginia
Peabody, Charles Jones..........................Georgia
Peabody, Royal Canfield.........................Georgia
Pearson, Dr. Henry..............................Alabama
Pearson, William H.........................North Carolina

Pegram, Henry...Virginia
Peirce, J. Champlin..Florida
Pendergast, J. Lynch....................................Maryland
Pendergast, Raymond W...............................Maryland
Penniman, Arthur W.....................................Maryland
Pennock, Jerome Humphrey...........................Maryland
Perkins, W. R...Virginia
Perry, Sidney R...Florida
Peters, John Egbert....................................Tennessee
Peters, John W..Mississippi
Peters, Ralph..Georgia
Pett, Charles E...Georgia
Pfeiffer, H. L..Maryland
Phillips, C. C...Virginia
Pickett, Dr. P. D..Louisiana
Platt, E. C...Alabama
Poling, William Heiskell.................................Virginia
Polk, Frank L...Tennessee
Poore, John G..Delaware
Pope, Ernest...Georgia
Posey, William T..Kentucky
Pou, Dr. Robert Edward...................................Georgia
Price, Floyd...Virginia
Priddy, Lawrence...Virginia
Primrose, John S.....................................North Carolina
Prince, W. B..Virginia
Pritchard, Hugh Jerymn.....................................Texas
Pritchard, Dr. William B ....North Carolina
Proskauer, Joseph M......................................Alabama
Pulley, Dr. W. J...Alabama
Purrington, William Archer...................District of Columbia

Quay, John W...Virginia
Quinlan, Dr. Joseph S..................................Maryland
Quinlan, Dr. T. A.......................................Maryland

Raby, R. Cornelius...Texas
Rady, George Hannon.....................................Virginia
Ragan, Adolphus...Texas
Raine, Thomas Chalmers..................................Virginia
Ramsay, Dick S..Kentucky
Randolph, Edward.......................................Tennessee

Ravenel, St. Julien.............................South Carolina
Rawlins, Albert Whiteley........................Delaware
Rawls, Dr. Reginald M...........................South Carolina
Reed, Morton Wales..............................Virginia
Reese, Dr. Robert Grigg.........................Virginia
Reeves, M. R....................................North Carolina
Reeves, Richard E...............................North Carolina
Reinecke, Wm....................................Kentucky
Reynolds, D. R..................................Maryland
Rice, Bruce L...................................Tennessee
Richards, Dr. John D............................Mississippi
Richardson, Edw. Randolph.......................Virginia
Richardson, J. B................................West Virginia
Richardson, Lt. Cmdr. L. C......................South Carolina
Riely, John W...................................Virginia
Riely, Lambert M................................Virginia
Riordan, James..................................South Carolina
Ritchie, Albert.................................Maryland
Rivers, Julian Charlton.........................South Carolina
Roach, James P..................................Mississippi
Roberts, Albert G...............................Georgia
Roberts, William W., Jr.........................Maryland
Robertson, Dr. J. A.............................Texas
Robinson, Arthur D..............................Virginia
Robinson, Eugene B..............................Georgia
Robinson, Powhatan R............................Virginia
Robinson, Uel M.................................North Carolina
Rogers, Richard Reid............................Kentucky
Rothschild, Simon F.............................Georgia
Rountree, Louis G...............................North Carolina
Rucker, Robert Hamilton.........................Kentucky
Russell, Faris R................................Tennessee
Russell, John Mosby.............................Virginia
Russell, Lindsay................................North Carolina
Russell, L. T...................................Mississippi
Ryan, Allan A...................................Virginia

Salmon, Ellwood C...............................Georgia
Sands, Tucker K.................................Virginia
Saunders, Wm. L.................................Georgia
Scales, Dr. Jefferson...........................North Carolina
Scarburgh, Robt. S..............................Virginia

Schley, Buchanan, Jr.............................Maryland
Schoen, William P................................Georgia
Seal, William Elmore.............................Virginia
Sebrell, Marvin P................................Virginia
Sefert, Clarence L...............................Alabama
Seidell, Charles F...............................Virginia
Sellars, Joseph B............................North Carolina
Sellers, H. Lee..................................Virginia
Selvage, Edwin...................................Maryland
Semple, Lorenzo..................................Alabama
Semple, T. Darrington............................Alabama
Sevier, Henry H.................................Tennessee
Shafer, J. Clem..................................Virginia
Sharretts, Edward P..............................Maryland
Sheild, Edwin....................................Alabama
Sheppard, Walter Clifton............................Texas
Sherwood, Elmer Clyde...........................Tennessee
Shields, Dr. Nelson T...........................Kentucky
Shipman, Andrew J...............................Virginia
Shotwell, Edward O'Neal..........................Alabama
Sim, John Robert................................Virginia
Sim, Robert Lee.................................Virginia
Simmonds, Graff W..............................Louisiana
Sinclair, Hon. G. B.............................Virginia
Sinclair, George Terry..........................Virginia
Sistrunk, J......................................Georgia
Sizer, Robert Ryland............................Virginia
Sizer, Thomas M.................................Virginia
Skinner, Frank E.............................North Carolina
Slade, Dr. Charles Blount........................Georgia
Slee, John B....................................Maryland
Slingluff, Upton................................Maryland
Smith, Edgeworth................................Maryland
Smith, Elijah P.................................Maryland
Smith, F. Hopkinson.............................Maryland
Smith, Dr. Harmon...............................Georgia
Smith, H. Blair................................Tennessee
Smith, Oscar W.................................Maryland
Smith, Otis.....................................Missouri
Smith, Philip M................................Kentucky
Smith, Terry.......................................Texas
Smith, William Mason........................South Carolina

Snead, R. J..Virginia
Snead, Udolpho..Kentucky
Snider, Leonard.....................................Mississippi
Snowden, Stephen L.............................South Carolina
Snyder, Jos. C.......................................Virginia
Somerville, Hon. Henderson M........................Alabama
Soria, Henry J......................................Louisiana
Speiden, Clement C...................................Virginia
Speiden, Ernest K....................................Virginia
Spencer, Thomas Pitman...............................Virginia
Sperry, Edward Chambers.......................South Carolina
Sperry, Joseph Austin................................Virginia
Spooner, Henry W.....................................Virginia
Sprigg, James Cresap.................................Virginia
Springs, Albert A. ....South Carolina
Stafford, Hartwell..................................Alabama
Staples, Robt. Tyler.................................Virginia
Stark, Wilkinson...................................Louisiana
Staton, Henry..................................North Carolina
Steel, W. J..Kentucky
Steele, R. Breckinridge..............................Kentucky
Stephenson, Dr. Junius W.............................Virginia
Stewart, Fenwick J. T....................District of Columbia
Stockell, Hon. V. H.................................Tennessee
Stoddart, John H....................................Alabama
Stokes, Elmore K....................................Alabama
Stoll, Charles H....................................Kentucky
Strother, William A...........................South Carolina
Stuart, Francis Lee...........................South Carolina
Stump, A. Welles..............................West Virginia
Sturgis, Thomas Steele...............................Virginia
Supplee, J. Frank...................................Maryland
Sussdorf, Louis A.............................South Carolina
Sussdorf, William H...........................South Carolina
Sutcliffe, A. Sidney..........................South Carolina
Sykes, George...Texas

Tabb, Henry A..Virginia
Talbert, Joseph T.................................Mississippi
Talbert, Walter W.................................Mississippi
Talley, Dr. W. W.....................................Virginia
Tannor, John...Virginia

Tate, Sterrett..Alabama
Taylor, Esten C...............................South Carolina
Taylor, Dr. Fielding L...............................Virginia
Taylor, Horace Russell...............................Kentucky
Taylor, James L......................................Florida
Taylor, Rupert......................................Arkansas
Taylor, Dr. Thomas M................................Kentucky
Taylor, Walter F.....................................Virginia
Tetard, Louis C......................................Missouri
Thompson, Burton.....................................Missouri
Thompson, Jefferson de Mont..........................Alabama
Thurston, John L.....................................Virginia
Tiedeman, Irvin B.............................South Carolina
Toby, Geo. Parmly..................................Louisiana
Towns, Charles B.....................................Georgia
Towns, Mirabeau L....................................Georgia
Trawick, Samuel W....................................Georgia
Treloar, Charles E.................................Louisiana
Trenholm, Frank...............................South Carolina
Trice, Mann..Georgia
Trussell, Arthur J..............................West Virginia
Tucker, James R.....................................Maryland
Tucker, St. George Brooke.............................Texas
Tull, Dr. Edward E..................................Maryland
Turlington, Edgar Eastwood....................North Carolina
Turnbull, V. E.......................................Florida
Turner, William C.............................South Carolina

Ullrich, Albert R......................................Texas

Vandiver, Almuth C...................................Alabama
VanWyck, Hon. Augustus........................South Carolina
VanWyck, William.....................................Virginia
Vick, Walker Whiting..........................North Carolina
Violett, Atwood....................................Louisiana

Walker, Byrd...Virginia
Walker, David L......................................Georgia
Walker, Frank M....................................Tennessee
Walker, Norman S.....................................Virginia
Walsh, Ossie J.....................................Tennessee
Walters, Edgar B.....................................Virginia

Walton, David E...................................Missouri
Ward, Horatio J...................................Kentucky
Ward, Samuel M., Jr............................South Carolina
Warriner, Arthur.................................Virginia
Warwick, Chas. P................................Virginia
Warwick, D. Branch.............................Virginia
Washington, George A..........................Tennessee
Washington, William deH........................Virginia
Waters, Thomas Jackson...................District of Columbia
Watkins, James L................................Tennessee
Watson, Archibald R............................Mississippi
Watson, James Henry, Jr......................Mississippi
Watson, Dr. S. P.............................South Carolina
Watts, Harry Dorsey............................Maryland
Watts, John J................................West Virginia
Waugh, Henry Proctor..........................Tennessee
Wayt, Dr. W. Baldwin..........................Virginia
Weathers, Niel A...............................Florida
Wedekind, Gustav C...........................Maryland
Weed, John W...................................Georgia
Weil, Henry G..................................Missouri
Weir, J. Campbell..............................Maryland
Weisiger, John N...............................Virginia
Welles, Frank Corday..........................Virginia
Wells, Crawford H..............................Virginia
Wells, Joseph R................................Missouri
Weslosky, Morris...............................Georgia
West, J. Terry................................Mississippi
Westmoreland, Dr. F. S.....................South Carolina
Whilden, William G........................South Carolina
Whipp, Paul C..................................Maryland
Whitcomb, Henry Donald........................Virginia
White, E. H....................................Maryland
White, John P..................................Maryland
White, Wm. K...................................Maryland
Whitfield, Edwin N...........................Mississippi
Whitlock, Bernard..........................North Carolina
Whitlock, Victor E.........................North Carolina
Wight, William A...............................Kentucky
Wilhoite, Joseph D.............................Tennessee
Wilkes, Nathaniel Robords......................Tennessee
Williams, Andrew Murray......................Mississippi

Williams, Frederic A..Georgia
Williams, George B..Missouri
Williams, James Oscar.......................................South Carolina
Williams, James R..North Carolina
Williams, Oscar F..Maryland
Williams, W. C., Jr...Virginia
Williamson, Frank...Virginia
Wilson, Bruce C..Maryland
Wilson, Butler Millard..Virginia
Wilson, E. Bright..Tennessee
Wilson, Hunter LeGrand..Tennessee
Wilson, John Alexander..Virginia
Wilson, Junius Pendleton..Virginia
Winslow, William Beverly..Kentucky
Witherspoon, Preston..Mississippi
Wofford, Charles P..Mississippi
Wolf, Ralph..Arkansas
Wolfe, W. Preston..Kentucky
Wood, Fern Manly...Alabama
Woodward, Christopher H. R.......................................Maryland
Woog, Henry..District of Columbia
Woolfolk, Joseph W..Georgia
Woolsey, Minthorne...Alabama
Worrall, Richard P...Kentucky
Wright, Charles Allen..Mississippi
Wylie, J. Caldwell..South Carolina
Wylie, Dr. R. H...South Carolina

Yoakum, B. F..Texas
Young, Thomas Sloan...Georgia

Zacharias, L. B..Maryland
Zion, Charles M...Virginia

NON-RESIDENT MEMBERS

Name	State of Birth or Descent	Address
Alfriend, Winter Woolfolk	Ga.	Atlanta, Ga.
Allen, Andrew Henderson	Va.	Hoosick Falls, N. Y.
Archbell, John Eborn	N. C.	Xanthi, Bulgaria
Baker, Capt. Charles T.	S. C.	New York, N. Y.
Baldwin, George J.	Ga.	Savannah, Ga.
Baldwin, Lorenzo M.	Fla.	Jacksonville, Fla.
Banister, Blair	Ala.	Memphis, Tenn.
Bell, Frank Martin	N. C.	Chicago, Ill.
Berg, Louis S.	Ga.	Paris, France
Bertie, Cecil E.	Va.	Philadelphia, Pa.
Brooke, Dandridge W.	Va.	Newark, N. J.
Brown, Joshua	Tenn.	Nashville, Tenn.
Bryan, James A.	N. C.	New Bern, N. C.
Buck, R. S.	Miss.	Montreal, Can.
Buck, Samuel Henry	Ky.	New York, N. Y.
Burgess, D. R.	Va.	Mobile, Ala.
Caldwell, A. B.	N. C.	Atlanta, Ga.
Campbell, D. Crowell	Ga.	Knoxville, Tenn.
Canup, Rev. M. Luther	N. C.	New York, N. Y.
Carr, Julian S.	N. C.	Durham, N. C.
Carson, J. A. G.	Md.	Savannah, Ga.
Claiborne, Rev. Dr. R. R.	Va.	New York, N. Y.
Clarke, James	Md.	Cumberland, Md.
Clifton, John W.	La.	Washington, D. C.
Colding, Dr. Henry S.	Ga.	Savannah, Ga.
Condon, Martin J.	Tenn.	Memphis, Tenn.
Crawford, Geo. Gordon	Ga.	Birmingham, Ala.
Crockett, Watkins	Tenn.	Nashville, Tenn.
Crump, James D.	Va.	Richmond, Va.
Cummins, George C.	Tenn.	Memphis, Tenn.
Curry, M. W.	Fla.	Key West, Fla.
Davis, Edward B.	Tenn.	Interlaken, N. J.
Davis, Westmoreland	Va.	Leesburg, Va.

Dinkins, Lynn H............	Miss..........	New Orleans, La.
Dox, Charles E.............	Va................	Chicago, Ill.
Drumheller, Jerome L.......	Tenn...........	Spokane, Wash.
Dwyer, Major Charles G......	Tex...........	New York, N. Y.
Echols, Lt. Col. Charles P.....	Ala..........	West Point, N. Y.
Edmonds, Richard H.........	Va............	Baltimore, Md.
Edwards, Edmund P.........	Ky.........	Schenectady, N. Y.
Ellyson, H. Theodore.........	Va............	Richmond, Va.
Farish, John B.............	N. C............	Denver, Col.
Flinn, Homer C............	Ga...............	Mobile, Ala.
Francis, Hon. David Rowland..	Ky............	St. Louis, Mo.
Frazier, J. Miller...........	Ky..........	New York, N. Y.
Gaines, Clement C...........	Va.........	Poughkeepsie, N. Y.
Gaines, Wm. Pendleton.......	Tex............	Austin, Texas
Garnett, Dr. A. Y. P.........	D. C.........	Washington, D. C.
Gillette, James E...........	Va...........	Belle Mead, N. J.
Glennon, James K...........	Ala..............	Mobile, Ala.
Goldsborough, R. E. L........	Md..........	New Orleans, La.
Goldsborough, Richard F......	Md..........	New Orleans, La.
Goldsborough, Winder E.......	Md.............	Denver, Col.
Gordon, Douglas H...........	Md............	Baltimore, Md.
Gossett, James P...........	S. C..........	Williamston, S. C.
Graham, Carroll B...........	Va...............	Chicago, Ill.
Gray, Leslie H.............	Ark...............	Orange, Va.
Grayson, John Watson........	Va..............	Bradford, Pa.
Hanger, Harry Baylor........	Va............	New York, N. Y.
Harahan, Wm. J............	Tenn............	Norfolk, Va.
Harby, Walter I...........	S. C...........	Sumter, S. C.
Heath, M. C...............	Ga............	Columbia, S. C.
Henry, C. S...............	Md............	Cambridge, Md.
Hester, Rev. St. Clair, D.D.....	N. C...........	Brooklyn, N. Y.
Hoffman, J. Milton...........	D. C....	San Luis Potosi, Mexico
Hoge, Charles C.............	D. C............	Hartford, Conn.
Horn, Rev. William M........	S. C.	New York, N. Y.
Hundley, Oscar R...........	Ala...........	Birmingham, Ala.
Hyde, Henry W............	Va............	Clearbrook, Va.
Innerarity, Lewis A. R........	Md............	Baltimore, Md.

Jackson, Hon. Wm. H.......... Tenn......... Ancon, Canal Zone
Jarnagin, William Nicholas..... Tenn.............. Chicago, Ill.
Johnson, B. F................ Va........... Washington, D. C.
Junkin, Francis T. A.......... Va............... Chicago, Ill.

Kable, Dr. John L............ Va........... Philadelphia, Pa.
Keep, O. H.................. Miss......... Mayersville, Miss.
Kendrick, John R............. Ga.......... Philadelphia, Pa.
Kennington, R. E............. Ga.............. Jackson, Miss.
Kirby, John Henry........... Tex............ Houston, Texas

Lamb, Lawrence............. Tenn......... Memphis, Tenn.
Lamberd, Charles E......... Md......... Clarksburg, W. Va.
Lanier, John F............... Ala............. St. Louis, Mo.
Lee, Gen. Joseph............ S. C......... Hampton, Va.
Lejeune, Col. John Archer...... La........... New York, N. Y.
Loveman, D. B.............. Tenn....... Chattanooga, Tenn.
Lloyd, Rt. Rev. Arthur Seldon.. Va........... New York, N. Y.
Lynah, James............... S. C......... Newburgh, N. Y.

McCready, Rev. W. G., D.D... Ky............ Brooklyn, N. Y.
McCreary, Hon. James B....... Ky............ Frankfort, Ky.
MacRae, Hugh............... N. C....... Wilmington, N. C.
Mahaffey, Capt. Birche O..... Tex........... Honolulu, H. I.
Minor, Wirt................. Va........... Portland, Ore.
Moore, William E............ Md........... Baltimore, Md.
Morehead, Dr. J. A.......... Va............ Salem, Va.
Murnan, Chas. Edw........... Va........... Allston, Mass.

Nelms, W. S................. Tex......... Georgetown, Texas
Nolley, Ralph F.............. Md........... Baltimore, Md.
Nydegger, Dr. James A........ Md........... Baltimore, Md.

Peck, Horace Sill............. Va........... Rochester, N. Y.
Penick, S. B................. Va........... Marion, N. C.
Polk, Anderson............. Tenn..... Roland Park, Maryland
Porter, John T.............. Del.............. Scranton, Pa.

Reed, Stanley F.............. Ky............ Maysville, Ky.
Rees, Henry E............... Ga........... Hartford, Conn.
Rice, Lieut. Arthur Hopkins, Jr. Miss............ Wash., D. C.
Ripley, Daniel............... Ala........... Houston, Texas

Samuels, Charles B............	Va................	Paris, France
Saulsbury, Willard............	Del.............	Wilmington, Del.
Scales, H. L.................	Tex..............	Dallas, Tex.
Scott, R. J..................	Ga...............	Atlanta, Ga.
Seagle, Rev. Nathan A., D.D...	N. C.............	New York, N. Y.
Sevier, Capt. Granville........	Tenn.......	Fort Hamilton, N. Y.
Seward, Dr. Walter M.........	Va...............	Triplet, Va.
Shepherd, Robert B..........	Va............	Nassau, Bahamas
Shine, Francis Eppes..........	Fla..............	Bisbee, Ariz.
Siler, Capt. J. F..............	Ala..............	Wash., D. C.
Simmons, Rev. James D........	Md..............	New York, N. Y.
Simpson, Earnest C...........	Tenn.......	New Haven, Conn.
Slicer, J. S..................	Va..............	Atlanta, Ga.
Smith, Charles Henry..........	Ga.........	East Pittsburgh, Pa.
Smith, Rev. Charles J.........	Va............	New York, N. Y.
Smyth, Ellison A.............	S. C...........	Greenville, S. C.
Spiller, Stuart M.............	Va...........	Shanghai, China
Stalnaker, Dr. Paul R.........	Tex..............	U. S. Navy
Staples, J. N., Jr............	N. C............	Boston, Mass.
Steele, Rev. J. Nevett.........	Md.........	East Hampton, L. I.
Stewart, Capt. H. C. H........	Md..........	Washington, D. C.
Stillman, James S.............	Ala...........	Catasauqua, Pa.
Stires, Rev. Ernest M., D.D....	Va............	New York, N. Y.
Sutter, Charles..............	Ky..............	St. Louis, Mo.
Symonds, Edmund Harvey.....	Ala.........	San Juan, Porto Rico
Thompson, Rev. Wm. J., D.D..	Md..............	Madison, N. J.
Tillman, Col. Samuel E........	Tenn.........	New York, N. Y.
Tison, William S..............	Ga..............	Savannah, Ga.
Waller, Edmund Putzel........	Va...........	Schenectady, N. Y.
Watts, Legh R................	Va............	Portsmouth, Va.
Whedbee, M. Manly...........	Md..............	London, Eng.
Wheeler, Major Joseph, Jr.....	Ala............	Fort Adams, R. I.
White, Col. John V............	Miss...........	Charleston, S. C.
Whitmore, B. Thos............	Md.............	Lakewood, N. J.
Williams, Dr. D. H............	Ala............	Knoxville, Tenn.
Williams, Major James M......	Ala...........	Fort Monroe, Va.
Williams, John Skelton,.......	Va.............	Richmond, Va.
Winship, Major Blauton.......	Ga.............	Wash., D. C.
Woodruff, L. Frank...........	Ga..............	Boston, Mass.

IN MEMORIAM

Since 1896

	DIED
AIKEN, WILLIAM MARTIN	1908
ALEXANDER, WALTER	1909
ALMOUR, JOHN C.	1911
ARD, PHILIP H.	1913
BAKER, GEORGE B.	1910
BALDWIN, C. C.	1897
BEATON, W. O.	1910
BLACK, JOHN F.	1912
BROWN, REV. JOHN W.	1900
BROWN, REV. PHILIP A. H.	1909
BROWNING, WILLIS	1914
BRUCE, LESLIE C.	1911
BYRD, ALFRED H.	1897
CARLISLE, HON. JOHN G.	1910
CARY, CLARENCE	1911
CASKIN, COL. THEODORE C.	1911
CASTLEMAN, BRECKINRIDGE	1912
CHAPMAN, DR. ROBERT FERGUSON	1912
CHILD, CHARLES F.	1906
CHILD, CHARLES TRIPLER	1902
CHILDS, WILLIAM WARD	1911
CLARK, J. SHEPHERD	1913
COLE, E. W.	1899
COLE, HUGH LAING	1898
COX, JENNINGS S.	1913
COXE, DR. DAVIES	1908
DENT, DR. EMMET C.	1906
DES PORTES, R. S.	1898
DEW, DR. J. HARVIE	1914
DICKINSON, COL. A. G.	1906

	DIED
DONIPHAN, JOHN V	1912
DUDLEY, EVANS	1910
DUNCAN, GEORGE E	1903
DUNHAM, BRADFORD	1908
DUNLAP, GEORGE H	1907
EARLE, LEWIS	1913
FALLIGANT, HON. ROBERT	1902
FITE, DR. C	1907
FOWLER, DR. GEORGE B	1907
GARDEN, HUGH R	1911
GOLSON, E. G	1903
GORDON, JAMES LINDSAY	1904
GRAY, DR. LANGDON C	1900
GRIMES, DR. G	1908
GUGGENHEIMER, RANDOLPH	1907
HALL, EDWIN B	1908
HANSON, MAJOR J. F	1910
HARDEN, HON. WILLIAM D	1898
HARRISON, BURTON N	1904
HARTLEY, DR. FRANK	1913
HENDERSON, WALTER H	1914
HIX, W. PRESTON	1911
HOLLAND, RALPH H	1911
HOPKINS, GUS C	1900
HOUSTON, W. B	1900
INGRAM, JOHN H	1906
JANIN, HENRY	1911
JARVIS, SAMUEL M	1914
JENKINS, REGINALD C	1910
JOHNSON, JAMES L	1906
JOHNSON, JOHN R	1898
KEENER, HON. WILLIAM A	1913
KRUTTSCHNITT, ERNEST B	1906
LANIER, REUBEN ROYAL	1902
LANKFORD, RICHARD D	1914
LATHAM, JOHN C., JR	1909
LEWIS, CHARLES E	1912
LIGON, DR. GREENWOOD	1911

	DIED
LINDSAY, HON. WILLIAM...................	1909
LOWNDES, LLOYD..........................	1905
MCCAY, J. RINGGOLD......................	1914
MCGUIRE, THOMAS J.......................	1912
MAGUIRE, FRANK Z........................	1910
MAITLAND, BURGWYN.......................	1912
MALLARD, WILLIAM J., JR.................	1902
MALLETT, JAMES F........................	1906
MALLETT, COL. PETER.....................	1907
MASON, JULIEN J.........................	1914
MAYO, JOHN C. C.........................	1914
MILES, W. PORCHET.......................	1899
MILLAR, HUGH GRAHAM.....................	1911
MOFFETT, JAMES A........................	1913
MONROE, JAMES R.........................	1912
MOREHEAD, COL. FRANKLIN C...............	1914
MORROW, DR. PRINCE A....................	1913
MOSES, ISAAC HARBY......................	1901
MOUNTJOY, C. A..........................	1913
NEVILLE, GEORGE WILDER..................	1914
NUNN, DR. R. J..........................	1910
NYE, THEODORE S.........................	1900
OLIVER, CHARLES KEMBLE..................	1910
PAGE, DR. R. C. M.......................	1898
PARRISH, WILLIAM PECK...................	1901
PARROTT, SAMUEL F.......................	1910
PATTESON, JAMES A.......................	1905
PATTESON, THOMAS A......................	1903
PAYNE, ARCHER LANGHORNE.................	1901
PEARCE, MORGAN..........................	1913
PHELAN, EDWARD F........................	1900
POLK, DR. J. M..........................	1904
POWELL, DR. S. D........................	1907
PRICE, BRUCE............................	1903
PRICE, PROF. THOMAS R...................	1903
QUARRIER, ARCHIE M......................	1900
QUINLAN, L. G...........................	1904
READ, ISAAC.............................	1908

	DIED
REED, WILLIAM M.	1899
RHETT, E. LOWNDES	1914
ROBB, J. HAMPDEN	1911
ROBBINS, GASTON A.	1902
ROBERTSON, TOURO	1899
ROUNTREE, ALBERT L.	1907
RUSSELL, WILLIAM HEPBURN	1911
SAUNDERS, HOWARD	1897
SCHENCK, SAMUEL G.	1906
SHARP, W. NEWTON	1909
SHEPPERSON, ALFRED B.	1911
SHORT, HENRY B.	1914
SIOUSSAT, WM. D.	1912
SMITH, BENJAMIN RUSH	1911
SPEIR, A. W.	1910
SPENCER, SAMUEL	1906
SPROUL, ARCHIBALD A.	1910
SWANN, JAMES	1903
SWEPSON, R. R.	1902
TAYLOR, MORTIMER F.	1903
THOMAS, SAMUEL	1903
THOMPSON, HUGH S.	1904
TILFORD, W. H.	1909
TOWSON, ALLAN S.	1908
TOY, JOSEPH A.	1901
TRENHOLM, W. L.	1901
WATSON, E. SCOTT	1902
WEIL, SOL. C.	1898
WHITE, OCTAVIUS A.	1903
WILSON, BENJAMIN LEE	1911
WILSON, RICHARD T.	1910
WINN, JASPER C.	1910
WOODWARD, JAMES T.	1910
WRENN, BEVERLY W.	1912

CPSIA information can be obtained
at www.ICGtesting.com
Printed in the USA
BVHW091230261118
534010BV00012B/541/P